PRAISE FOR

MW00782218

"Fall seven times. Stand up eight
sible. But God makes it possible, and Cory gives you a structured, proven approach to *rise* after life knocks you down and *go* "up and to the right" with confidence. Every recommended step is reinforced with real-world examples from the lives of leaders with whom you can identify. Get *Rise and Go*, get back on your feet, and get moving."

—**CHRIS BOLINGER**, entrepreneur and author of *Daily Strength for Men* and *52 Weeks of Strength for Men*

"Life is hard and learning to lead well in the middle of life's messes is even harder! *Rise and Go* is a fantastic and moving, real life story of overcoming struggle as a result of his focus on faith and pure determination to find God's true purpose and meaning for his life! This story will motivate anyone that is struggling with life and the call to lead stronger and more effectively for your family, team or business. I'm so thankful to Cory for courageously putting his story out there because there isn't one of us that's immune to struggle and hardship and it's stories of success like this that give us hope. And, for some, stories like Cory's help us find our way out of the darkness and into the light!"

—**JASON LIPPERT**, President and CEO of LCI Industries, a Fortune 1000 company

"To have a forward advancing life, you will get knocked down from time to time. I have been knocked down a lot, especially these last couple of years. God calls us to get back up. Cory has worked with leaders I know to help them get back up and navigate the challenges of leadership and life. Cory has a deep well to draw from with his strong faith foundation and business world experience. He is a good man and a guide to learn from."

—**BRIAN TOME**, founding and Senior Pastor of Crossroads Church, author, and host of 'The Aggressive Life' podcast

"*Rise and Go* is packed with powerful principles, insights and stories to help you become a transformational leader. You will be challenged and encouraged as Cory shares with authenticity and transparency about his own leadership experience. *Rise and Go* provides quick and insightful tools you can immediately implement into the your day-to-day life. It is a book you will want to keep nearby as you will reference often on your leadership journey."
— **DAN BRITTON**, Chief Field Officer of Fellowship of Christian Athletes, and author of seven books including *One Word*

"Wonderfully wise!! In this book, Cory Carlson has done a masterful job at creating an experience for leaders – the leader in *all* of us, he suggests! – that is deeply practical and impactful with ample tools for daily life. This should be in the library of regularly-referenced books of anyone who wants to impact change and live a life of deep communion with God and neighbor."
— **SARAH DAVISON-TRACY** - author, speaker, founder (Seeds of Exchange & Rooted and Beloved)

"When Cory asked me to read and review *Rise and Go* unbeknownst to him, I was at one of the lowest points of my life; my career was influx, I was in the middle of a health crisis and I discovered I could not answer the question, "what do you want". For me *Rise and Go* has become my daily playbook for leading myself, my business and my home. While a Christian leader's journey is never finished, *Rise and Go* has become my oasis on that Journey."
— **RON KITCHENS**, best selling author of *Community Capitalism* and *Uniquely You*

"Honest and fruitful. Cory becomes your personal Coach - keeping you rooted in what's really important and your eyes fixed forward."
— **QUINCEY FOX**, Regional Vice President, PFS Investments Inc.

"Even the strongest men and women get beaten down by the grind of life from time to time. We all get knocked to the mat. But it's the resolve we show and the things we learn while we are down that make us true leaders. *Rise and Go* will help everyone to stand up once again with a renewed passion and confidence to lead."

—**ROCKY BOIMAN**, ESPN College Football Analyst, radio host 700WLW, author of *Rocky's Rules*

"I was feeling unsettled in both my personal and professional life. Then I read and did the work of *Rise and Go* leading to a break-through moment where I realized I had been leaning on circumstance-dependent situations for peace. *Rise and Go* redirected me on the right path forward, a path dependent on intimacy with God and intimacy with my husband. Thank you Cory!"

—**BECKY POMERLEAU**, Director, SOX Program and Believe ERG Co-lead at PayPal

"Leading is tough. The 'bounce-back' is what counts. What Cory has built here will help you not just push past difficult days blindly, but instead respond to them from a position of humble strength. I encourage you to use *Rise and Go* to become a truly healthy, standout leader in today's burnout culture."

—**KURT KERSEY**, Founder of Thirty21 & The Grown Man Project

"I found Cory Carlson's book to be incredibly timely for me. He gives real, raw, incredibly practical, and theologically sound advice in a very digestible format. I love the example narratives that pull you into the biblical stories and his own personal experiences. These helped tremendously in applying the truths of the book. I'd recommend this book to any leader who is serious about pursuing God — amid life's challenges, no matter where He may lead."

—**RASHAWN COPELAND**, Founder and CEO, Blessed Media, Author of *No Turning Back*

"*Rise and Go*, is very transparent with tremendous humility and is an amazing read. I greatly enjoyed it and was impacted by it! Life has many twists and turns and knocks down every leader at times. God calls us to rise up, but how do we do that? This book is a proven system to succeed. This playbook will assist you in what to do and where to turn. Cory Carlson's book, *Rise and Go* is a must read!! It will be life changing for you."
    —MARK WHITACRE, PhD., Executive Director of t-factor

"*Rise and Go* is overwhelmingly inspirational while providing an essential toolkit for leaders to effectively conquer challenges at work and at home. Cory melds scripture, stories from himself and other leaders, and reflection exercises to instill confidence and conviction while motivating the reader to overcome obstacles and continue moving forward. This book belongs on the bookshelf of any leader that relishes the messiness of leadership, takes calculated risks, and seeks to learn and grow from their experiences."
    —JEFF GILKINSON, CEO of Auveco

"*Rise and Go* is a collection of stories, ideas, and examples that will challenge you to keep going. It's perfect for anyone who believes they are called to elevate others and live out their God-Given purpose."
    —JOHN EADES, CEO of LearnLoft,
    author of *Building the Best*

"*Rise and Go* is packed with biblical truth, relatable stories, and tangible exercises that facilitate change at a heart level. The content is impactful for leaders at all levels of an organization and inspires action!"
    —MANDY ROBINSON, Sr. Director of Engineering
    & Technology at J.B. Hunt Transport Services, Inc

"Too often business leader's *home game* isn't as good as their *away game*. I love Cory's commitment to making sure we're better at home so we can be better at work. I am grateful Cory has published another resource for business leaders to use as they encounter the ups and downs of leadership, both at home and work."

—**JUSTIN FORMAN**, Executive Director
of Faith Driven Entrepreneur

"As I read *Rise and Go*, I found myself taking notes and rereading various sections to make sure I fully captured the detailed lessons Cory offers in each chapter. He takes us on a journey of faith turned into action; I felt like I was sitting next to him in the front seat as we drove across the country, as he shared his story (can't wait for the audio version!). Cory challenges us at the beginning of each chapter, then shares simple steps to demonstrate the leadership traits he brings to life. Cory's use of scripture makes this a must read for anyone struggling with their faith, as a spouse, parent, or leader. Spiritual warfare is real and *Rise and Go* will arm you for battle by teaching you how to talk to God and build your life around Him, helping you keep your temporal journey in perspective and find peace, even during the most challenging times."

—**PETE DURAND**, CEO of Cruxible Partners

"At some point in their leadership journey, every leader will face tremendous obstacles and lose their footing. The good news is that getting knocked down doesn't have to be the end of the story. In *Rise and Go*, there is a blueprint not only in how to respond, but ultimately how to flourish in the face of adversity. Cory does a wonderful job of demonstrating his own path and then allowing the reader to mark their own journey for replenishment and action. This is a great resource to create and maintain positive momentum and allow leaders to multiply their talents."

—**JUDD SEMINGSON**, CEO of Community Clinic NWA

"Cory Carlson is a successful Executive Coach who has "been through the wars" and knows from which he speaks. In *Rise and Go* he combines real-life stories from the Bible with those of successful leaders today to help us understand how we can be genuine and effective in our leadership roles. *Rise and Go* makes clear that becoming a great leader is a day-to-day journey and the Action Steps at the end of each chapter will guide you to make that journey well. Cory's down-to-earth style and practical experience provides all the tools you need to be a great leader."
—**RICK L. STEPHENS**, Founder of Horizon
Hobby Inc., author of *In Plane Sight*

"Need both a push and a dose of inspiration to take charge of your life? Then *Rise and Go* by Cory Carlson is for you. Cory's pragmatic, personal and relatable stories along with his faith-driven principles and straightforward action plan will give you the confidence to create the life you deserve."
—**AMY CONNOR**, CEO/Owner of CMO-OnLoan

"A leader is not defined by a title. Everyone leads someone. As a leader looking to integrate personal, professional, and spiritual, *Rise and Go* is a great place to start. This book will not only advance your leadership but anyone who comes in contact with you. Cory shares his story of triumph and many other leaders' stories that have been battle tested. Each chapter provides stories, action steps, prayer and supporting scripture."
—**KENDRA RAMIREZ**, CEO of
Kendra Ramirez Digital Agency

"Even better than the book is the author who wrote it! Which gives the book that much more credibility. Cory is a man who's walked through the fires of life, fought through each one and has come out the other side with more strength, vision and heart to help others do the same. *Rise and Go* is invaluable inspiration and application as to how you can also overcome each challenge."

—**BRANDON SCHAEFER**, Founder
and CEO of Five Capitals

"Cory has an amazing ability to make complex learnings simple by communicating them in a chapter by chapter, digestible style. He takes the knowledge that he has accumulated over the years, connects it to scripture and is able to share his wisdom through his humble failures and inspiring successes. This is a must read for anyone looking for continuous improvement in every area of their life."

—**BRYAN KAISER**, founding partner and Chief
Business Development Officer of Vernovis

"As a business owner I know how easy it is to get lost in the day to day minutia of work and to lose site of the excitement, passion and gifts which the Lord has endowed us with. If you're anything like me and you found yourself in this rut from time to time, then *Rise and Go* is a must read. It will walk you down the path of reigniting and rediscovering your passion for work, family and Christ."

—**DR. RAYMOND BONOMO,**
owner of Bonomo Periodontics

"As the great philosopher Iron Mike Tyson once said, 'everyone has a plan until they get punched in the mouth.' Cory Carlson's *Rise and Go* is a roadmap for getting off the mat, and back in the fight. Cory's words aren't based in theory, but on his real life journey and expertise as a coach. Read this book — and get ready to rise and go!"

—**CHUCK MINGO**, CEO & Founder, Courageous Love and Teaching Pastor, Crossroads Church

RISE
AND GO

How to Get Back Up with Courage and
Move Forward with Confidence

CORY M. CARLSON

Rise and Go: How to Get Back Up with Courage and Move Forward with Confidence
Published by Cloud Rider Publishing
Cincinnati, OH

ISBN: 978-1-7337671-1-8
BUSINESS & ECONOMICS / Personal Success

QUANTITY PURCHASES: Companies, professional groups, clubs, and other organizations may qualify for special terms when ordering quantities of this title. For information, email cory@corymcarlson.com.

CLOUD RIDER
PUBLISHING

DEDICATION

*To my amazing and supportive wife, Holly, and our
three incredible kids—Kiley, Kamdyn, and Kaleb:*

*Thank you for encouraging me in the challenging
moments that inspired this book.*

*I pray that I will be there for you during
your hard moments, as well.*

I love you.

CONTENTS

Part 3—GO: Move Forward with Confidence

FOREWORD

I couldn't believe how fast it happened. Within just a few days, my team and I went from not knowing how to spell coronavirus, to the pandemic forcing us to cut 80% of our staff of 150.

I had already spent five years in the business—one as consultant, three as CEO, and now one as Executive Chairman—and I was tired. I was weary. And there was a part of me that wanted to give up, cash in our chips, and get out.

But then I was reminded of the Apostle Paul's words in Ephesians 2:10: "For we are God's handiwork, created in Christ Jesus to do good works, which God prepared in advance for us to do." A lot of people assume that when Paul says "good works" he's talking exclusively about evangelism or giving money to the poor. But the Greek word Paul uses literally means "work, task, and employment." In other words, the work leaders do Monday through Friday that is aligned with God's Word and contributes to human flourishing *is part of the very purpose of your salvation.*

I knew that our business was "good work." We were creating jobs that allowed low-wage workers and their families to thrive. We were solving a real problem in the world and serving our customers through the ministry of excellence. We were "winning the respect of outsiders" (see 1 Thessalonians 4:12) and opportunities to share the gospel. Clearly it wasn't the time to lie down and die. It was the time to rise up and go!

This book wasn't available to me during that crisis. But do I ever wish it would have been!

There is no shortage of books for leaders who have been knocked down. But this one is different in two important ways. First, this book is based on God's Word—the only foundation that can withstand life's greatest storms (see Matthew 7:24-27). Second, this book is *uber*-practical. Cory doesn't just tell you what to do, he *shows you how to do it*, culminating in your own "Rise and Go Manifesto" which you'll come back to time and time again.

The world can't afford for godly leaders to stay on the sidelines. So get off the mat and get into this book. It's time to *Rise and Go!*

JORDAN RAYNOR
Bestselling author of *Redeeming Your Time,*
Master of One, and *Called to Create*

PART 1

KNOCKED DOWN

When All Seems Lost

1

THE STARTING POINT

Who Is This Book For?

This book is for leaders. That includes you. Even if you don't think of yourself as a leader. If there's anybody in your life who follows your directions or recommendations—whether that's a kid, an employee, a client, or a friend—then this book is for you.

Leadership is hard. There are days when we don't feel like motivating or inspiring anyone. Heck, we sometimes wake up feeling tired and discouraged ourselves, so how can we motivate anybody else? We all have our own doubts and insecurities about our lives and the directions we're headed. We may wonder, too, if we're even doing the right things to develop those we lead and help them reach their full potential.

There are also days when the people we're leading don't do a good job of following! This could be a child who throws a temper tantrum, a prospect who rejects our business proposal, or an employee who isn't showing up to work on time. It can be anyone or anything.

This book is for the leader who, from time to time, gets knocked down but wants to get back up. That means it's for every leader. It's for me. It's for you.

It's time for us to rise and go.

THE INFAMOUS TACO NIGHT

About five years ago, I was at a surprise fortieth birthday party for my wife, Holly, which was being held at a fun bar and restaurant in downtown Cincinnati. The party was underway, and everyone was having a blast, dancing and talking. Appetizers and finger foods started to arrive in our private room, so I decided it was time to stop mingling for a while and eat a couple of tacos.

I grabbed my first taco and started to move it toward my mouth to take a bite, but when it got there: *BAM*! The taco smashed up against my mouth and collapsed like an accordion!

What? What just happened? I wondered. *Did my mouth not open? Did my brain forget to tell my mouth to open?* And of course: *Did anyone else see that?*

Perplexed, confused, and still hungry, I tried again. This time, I moved very slowly, with more deliberation. As the taco approached my face, I tried to open my mouth as wide as possible, but I could not open it very wide at all. I could not fit the taco inside my mouth!

In the following weeks, I learned that I had temporomandibular joint disorder, or TMD. According to the Johns Hopkins Medicine website, TMD is a disorder of the jaw muscles and joints that connect a person's jaw to their skull. The main cause of this disorder can be "excessive strain on the jaw joints and the muscle group that controls chewing, swallowing, and speech." This strain may be due to something called *bruxism,* which is "the habitual, involuntary clenching or grinding of teeth."[1]

---

1   "Temporomandibular Disorder (TMD)," Johns Hopkins Medicine, https://www.hopkinsmedicine.org/health/conditions-and-diseases/ temporomandibular-disorder-tmd.

At the time, I had never heard of TMD, but I've since learned that it is common. However, although it is frequently caused by chronic issues, TMD can often be resolved in a few months or even weeks.

My own TMD didn't go away on its own. In my efforts to get rid of it, I got a mouth guard to wear at night. I also had a few acupuncture treatments and some upper back and head massages. I even did some exercises at home. By doing all these things, I was able to resolve my TMD in about four months.

However, as in most cases, when something needs to be fixed, it is best to not just fix the surface-level problem. It's always best to determine the root cause of the problem and fix that! This was the case with my TMD.

In fact, the cause of my TMD that memorable night eating tacos is a significant part of my life's story.

WHY WAS I STRESSED?

At that time in my life, I was working as President of Sales for a national company that provided building foundation and infra-structure repair services. I was part of the executive team, and our company was owned by a private equity firm. For those who are not familiar with the private equity space, private equity firms buy companies with the intention of improving their processes and profitability, and then selling them again at a profit three to five years later. The night of my taco wake-up call came right after my executive team and I had spent much of the previous year preparing for a company sale that, ultimately, did not happen.

There were four of us on the company's executive team: the CEO, COO, CFO, and myself. Together, we had prepared our company story and our future growth plans, which we compiled into a book and presentation that we delivered to eleven different private equity firms. (By the way, this process was a hard and grueling process. But it's also been one of my favorite processes I've ever engaged in during my career, thanks to the experience and the increased business acumen I gained as a result of those efforts.)

After our presentations were done, we received offers from a handful of companies and eventually chose the one we were most interested in working with over the next few years. We agreed that we would be bought by this one company.

When a person buys a home, there is a due diligence period, during which the buyer gets a home inspection and can change his or her mind about a sale. There's a similar due diligence period in the business world. In our case, our prospective buyers decided that they had questions about the strength and duration of patents that were key to our company's successful operation. As a result, on about day forty-five of the sixty-day due diligence period, the buyer backed out.

To make matters worse, because that one buyer had changed their mind, the other buyers decided they were no longer interested in their original offer. So we couldn't sell the company for the desired amount. Without a sale in the foreseeable future, our private equity owners decided that they wanted to turn their focus to improving profitability in the short term. From the private equity owner's perspective, the best way to improve short-term profitably was to prune the lower performing areas, instead of spending more time and money to make them profitable. This meant that we had to both terminate underperforming sales members and shut down underperforming territories.

Now, I do not enjoy terminating people. However, as stressful as that task was, it was not the main source of my stress at that time in my life. My greatest stress was coming from a tension I felt over whether I wanted to keep working for that company—or, for that matter, for any company in corporate America.

You see, I had hired an executive coach a few years earlier, and I was loving the coaching process. I could see that it was impacting not only my life, but also the lives of those I led. I had been talking with our sales reps about purpose over profit, about the importance of dating their spouses, being intentional with their kids, and getting to the gym. We'd discussed the importance of making time for solitude, ways to handle conflict and rejection, elevating their mindsets, and so much more.

Best of all, it was working. We had begun to focus on the whole person instead of just the sales numbers, and this had yielded better results for the company as well! Because I knew how the coaching content had changed my life, and because I was now seeing it change my thirty-person sales force, I was now itching to do coaching myself, as a full-time job, in order to impact even more business leaders.

And that was the source of my stress!

How, I wondered, was I going to make executive coaching and speaking a full-time job? It didn't seem to make sense for me to leave my current position. As President of Sales, I was earning very good money, the most I ever had ever made. My family's health insurance was paid for by the company, and we were in a place where my wife didn't have to work. To be honest I was comfortable. I knew the routine of working in corporate America, and there was this sense of comfort of having a Civil Engineering degree working in a field I knew so well. Whereas, if I left corporate America for coaching, it would be new and uncomfortable territory. Plus, I'd always thought of myself as a corporate guy. Why would a corporate guy leave a corporate job?

The thought of trading in my high salary, great role, and responsibility for a starting role as a coach with zero clients felt more than just daunting and stressful. It felt outright foolish! I was also father of three young kids—Kiley, Kamdyn, and Kaleb—who at the time were eleven, seven, and three years old. I kept hearing all these thoughts in my head:

You can't leave all that money and security when you have a young family.

You can't throw away your Civil Engineering degree and

MBA to go do executive coaching.

There are already a ton of coaches out there!

Once you leave your industry you can never go back.

Still, I couldn't stop thinking about the idea of becoming a coach. I was drawn to the idea of helping people get better not just at work, but also at home and in life.

This ping-pong chorus of "should I stay or should I go" continued in my mind for several months. Then on Sunday, August 14, 2016, I heard a message at our church, Crossroads Church, in which people were encouraged to fast from something (food, social media, etc.). During the time we would normally engage in that activity, we were urged to go to God in prayer instead, with the hope of hearing from Him about the next steps to take concerning a problem we were facing.

With my career decision weighing heavily on me, I was "all in" to do this fasting exercise. I chose to fast from alcohol for the week. That day, my wife and I talked and prayed about the issue. We both wanted to get clarity about my job situation, as we were both tired of the tension and stress of not knowing what to do.

GETTING CLARITY

The very next morning, I called Aaron, our CFO, as I did every week. He and I were in the practice of speaking every Monday at 8:30 a.m., as I was sharing with him directly some of the coaching tools I had been using with my sales team.

When Aaron answered, he immediately put the phone on speaker mode and said, "Dick is here with us as well." Well, I knew exactly what that meant! Today's call would not be a coaching and discipling call. Instead, it would be *my* termination call! Dick was our COO, and it was my turn to get fired. I had known this was an inevitable result if we continued reducing our sales force and territories. After all, if you fire enough sales reps, eventually you no longer need a President of Sales!

I was so much at peace during this conversation that Aaron and Dick both commented that I sounded like I was in a good mood. I proceeded to tell them about the previous twenty-four hours, about how I had been praying for clarity concerning my job, and about how their call was an answer to that prayer. Granted, I never thought that answer would come the very next day!

As I hung up the phone, I was excited. Yes, I was also scared; however, I was ready to get started! Truth be told, I probably would never have quit my corporate executive job and started a coaching career if I hadn't gotten that nudge. The corporate identity, the high salary, the fancy title, my fear of starting a new career at forty years old, and the job security that came with working for a big company, all worked together to make me feel like I couldn't walk away. I had needed to be fired to start my new career. And that's exactly what had happened.

50/50

By the time all this happened, God had already been preparing me for what was to come. At one point during the previous few months as I wrestled with this tension, I sat down and had a quiet time with God that helped shape my future thinking.

During this quiet time, I pleaded for God's help and asked for clarity about whether I should stay in the President of Sales role or launch a coaching business. While I was praying and journaling, I heard what sounded like audible voice to me, say "50/50."

"What?" I asked God. "What does 50/50 mean? What are the two 50s?" And then I waited for the answer, which did not immediately come.

In the following days, as I sat with the idea of 50/50, I experienced a sense of peace and feeling of clarity that this next chapter of my life would involve two jobs: each of which would take up 50 percent of my professional time and provide 50 percent of my

income. One of these jobs would be coaching. I had no idea what
form the other 50 percent would take.

I shared these insights with Brandon Schaefer, who has been
my executive coach for the last nine years. Brandon lives in South
Carolina. But unbeknownst to me, at the time he also happened to be
coaching a business owner named Chris Hartenstein, who lived in the
same city as me: Cincinnati. Yet Chris and I did not know each other.

Chris had a business named Hartco and a father-son ministry
named The New Frontier. Both were growing, and Chris was at
a point where he needed some help. He was interested in hiring
someone to help with the sales and marketing of Hartco. If this
individual could also help with the ministry, so much the better. So
Brandon introduced Chris and me in case there was an opportunity
for us to work together and help each other in that season.

After meeting together four different times, Chris and I came to
an agreement, and thanks to God's provision and Chris's support,
I began to work with him just as my severance package was about
to run out. God's timing can be stressful when we want to have a
clear plan laid out before us. Yet so often, that provision comes just
in time. This was exactly how it happened for me.

Although working at Hartco didn't fully add up to 50 percent
of my corporate salary, it made up 50 percent of what I needed at
that time in my life. The wisdom I gained while working for Chris
has contributed significantly to who I am today as a father, as a
husband, and most importantly, as a man whose identity is based
on being a son of God.

As for the other 50 percent, I started my coaching business the
very day I was terminated. Thanks to God's provision, by the time
my four-month severance package was over, I had ten paying clients
who had each signed up for a monthly coaching retainer. Although
this did not add up to 50 percent of my corporate salary, I had
enough momentum to feel convinced that I'd made the right move.

Over the next three years, with Chris's encouragement and
support, I reduced my time at Hartco as my coaching business grew.

What began as a roughly 50/50 split in late 2016 developed into a 75/25 division of time and resources (75 percent coaching and speaking business, 25 percent Hartco). By January 2020, the split was more like 90/10. Throughout those years, I spent a significant amount of my prayer and quiet time reflecting on this transition and talking to God about various aspects of it, including the speed at which it was happening—or, as I sometimes pointed out to God, not happening! I also had many conversations with wise counselors in my life, including Brandon and Chris.

By the beginning of 2020, there was significant momentum behind my coaching and speaking business. In fact, thanks to God's provision, the business had grown so much that I was bringing in nearly the same monthly income I had at the corporate job I was terminated from in 2016! I felt confident I was heading in the right direction. By this point, 65 percent of my business's revenue came from coaching business leaders and 35 percent came from speaking engagements.

I had faith God had been behind the whole transition, thanks to the timing of my termination from my former job, the provision of a severance package from that job, the unfolding of the 50/50 bi-vocational job split, and my business's ongoing momentum.

So after much prayer and counsel, Holly and I, plus our three kids (who were sixteen, twelve, and eight years old at the time) took yet another leap of faith. Making the choice to walk away from the comfortable feeling of having an employer who would provide our insurance—and pay me a salary that covered our bills—we jumped, as a family, 100 percent into my coaching and speaking business.

The day of our leap was March 1, 2020.

2

A NEW SOURCE OF STRESS

Why You Should Read This Book

When we decided that I would become a full-time coach and speaker, the conditions around me had been like a series of green lights. Within a couple weeks, everything changed.

COVID-19 had already begun to arrive in the United States, and now it was quickly becoming a global pandemic. Experts were working to try to reduce the spread and impact of the virus. Some of these efforts included the implementation of travel restrictions, face mask requirements, and quarantines that kept people at home. Additionally, many companies began to implement work-from-home policies. As a result of these efforts, all my speaking engagements were cancelled nearly overnight. Just two weeks after my launch into full-time coaching and speaking, 35 percent of my business revenue instantly vanished!

My speaking engagements weren't the only casualties. I'd also had a few business development trips lined up, including upcoming workshops in Washington DC and Kansas City. Those trips had to be cancelled too.

Needless to say, I was scared and frustrated.

At that moment, no one had any idea what lay ahead. Would the restrictions last a couple of weeks? A few months? There were rumors that the travel shutdown could last until the end of the year, as other countries were extending their mandates due to the virus's impact in their countries.

I'd lost 35 percent of my income when my speaking engagements were cancelled. Now, what would happen to the 65 percent that came from coaching business leaders? I wondered:

Would my coaching clients start to drop out as their companies moved to cut expenses?

Did this spell the end of my recently launched, full-time coaching and speaking business?

Would I have to go find a corporate job?

Would I even be able to find a job during the pandemic, if I tried?

Processing these questions sent me into a tailspin. In addition to everyday concerns about family finances, there was also the fact that my oldest child, Kiley, was then a sophomore in high school, so fears of future college expenses were also starting to weigh on me.

I continued to wonder: Had I missed a signal from God? Had He been telling me in February to delay and I'd missed it? Had I jumped into my own thing too early? Was this just another time in my life that I acted not out of wisdom, but out of impatience? I wasn't sure if or where I'd run off the course God had laid out for me. I longed for answers, and I knew where I was most likely to find them.

TAKING IT TO GOD

In recent years, both my desire to have quiet time with God each day and my discipline for making it happen had grown. Now let's be clear, my quiet times weren't perfect. Plus, there were days when I missed having a quiet time at all. But in the months leading into this situation, I'd been in a good place. I'd been learning more about the Bible and was growing closer to God.

However, when the mandates were implemented and my revenue vanished, my daily quiet time with God became even longer. The difference was, this time I wasn't focused on learning more about the Bible and God, like I had been in the past. Instead, I was pleading for help. Pleading for answers.

There were days when I prayed on my knees in desperation. There were days when I was angry. There were days when I felt hopeless and numb. Days I got emotional.

My journal entries from these days are pretty telling and show how this situation was affecting every area of my life. Doubt was creeping in, not just about my current situation but also about my future. I was discouraged to be in my mid-forties and not "have it all figured out." I was beating myself up over having potentially made a terrible mistake by leaving corporate America.

These journal excerpts from early March 2020 clearly document the mental roller coaster I found myself on. Perhaps you were feeling much the same way, around the same time.

> March 21: *Lord, I need you. I need confidence. I need momentum. I need some wins. Lord, what can I do now to get some wins?*

I was certain that what I needed at the time was a little bit of success. Well, you can see by my next journal entry that those wins did not come! If you're a business owner, not getting wins in your business can affect all areas of your life. Your confidence is affected, your energy, your hope, and so much more. This was certainly my experience. A subsequent journal entry notes my discouragement.

> March 23: *Lord, I need you. I am just beat down. Tired and frustrated. Business seems down and out.*

A following entry continues down this path and also starts to show the heaviness of desperation I was feeling.

> March 25: *God, I am really trying to slow down my mind. I had such a panic or rush feeling in the past week about how I had to grow the business or else. A lot of it was out of comparison—please forgive me. A lot of it out of fear— please forgive me!*

According to John 10:10, the devil comes "to steal and kill and destroy." As my journal entries show, the devil was doing just that. He was stealing any joy I might have felt over taking the leap of faith and going full time into coaching. He was killing my hopes and dreams about growing my coaching and speaking business. He was destroying any momentum I still had left.

But I wasn't just scared for my family's finances and the future of my business. I was also frustrated. A lot of my frustration was directed at myself. *Did I misread what I thought were signs from God?* I wondered. *Should I have waited longer?*

A lot of my frustration, though, was directed at God. I'd felt sure that God was sending me signs that I should go into coaching and speaking full-time. To be honest—and I know this is shallow to say—I'd even thought that because I was being obedient and because I was also going "all in" on doing Kingdom work (since a lot of my coaching is faith-based), God would financially reward me.

However, that was not the case. Not only was my career move *not* proving to be lucrative, but my business was also losing momentum. As the month went on, my journal entries expand on my feelings of frustration and anger with God and show signs of a growing feeling that if things were to ever turn around, I'd have to be the one to make it happen!

> March 27: *Lord, this is my beef and frustration—if it is up to me, I get it done. For example, I recorded five podcasts! However, if it involves you, it takes too long. Why? I can't tell whether you are saying "no," "not now," or just developing character.*

Ouch! Probably not my finest day with God in my quiet time, however the inner struggle I was reporting was real. Maybe you can relate to feeling that something will get done only if *you* do it. On some days when I pray, I talk with God about something that I want to happen—for example, that I'll get a new client, that a situation will be resolved, or that someone will be healed—and it doesn't happen that day, or even that week. In that moment, I imagine I can act and nudge things along better than God.

The following entry was written in huge letters and circled multiple times in my journal:

> April 1, 2020: *What am I supposed to do?*

I was pleading for God to answer my questions. I was pleading for God to help me.

WHY I WROTE THIS BOOK

I am guessing that you can relate to these feelings from my journal entries in March and April of 2020. I am also confident that there have been other times in your life when you felt defeated, discouraged, and maybe even abandoned by God, just like I did. Maybe you experienced a problem with your job, a struggle in a relationship, a challenging health diagnosis, or just the feeling of wandering aimlessly through life. These feelings can show up in any area in life. When they do, we often don't know where to turn. But there is a source of help available to us. Although it did not come immediately, God *did* provide an answer to my journaled question: "What am I supposed to do?"

That answer is what I want to share with you. Spoiler alert, God did not give me a silver bullet answer outlining everything I was supposed to do. Silver bullet answers rarely exist. But God *does* help us. In Psalm 119:105 David says, "Your word is a lamp to my feet and a light to my path."

God doesn't present us with a multi-step plan. Rather, He gives us a little light and shows us the next possible steps to take. The truth is, if God gave us a five-year strategy plan, then many of us would say, "Goodbye God. See you in five years!" and go about our business. However, God wants a relationship with us. By giving us the next step and not a whole plan, He keeps us coming back to Him.

In my case, God spoke to me through various promptings that helped me see what I should do next. This book contains those promptings that He used to mold and shape me over one circumstantially difficult year to become a better husband, father, leader, and follower of Christ. The Bible verses, tools, and stories in this book are what kept me going each day.

On days when I woke up feeling defeated, I would come across one of the verses identified in this book, and it would help reorient me and get me back on my feet. In this way, God helped me to regain the confidence and motivation I needed to keep serving my clients, to search for new business prospects, and to intentionally relate with my family instead of giving in to discouragement, sitting on the couch, and aimlessly scrolling on my cell phone.

God brought these resources into my life at just the right time to give me a new perspective. We all have days when we think we are the only one facing battles. But other people encounter battles too—and often theirs are even worse. These tools reminded me of that fact, gave me hope that I could win my own battle, and shifted my mindset so that I saw myself not as a hopeless victim but a powerful victor.

As a result, I didn't just survive a challenging season. I also became stronger spiritually, mentally, relationally, and even financially.

OVERCOMING DOUBTS AND FINDING STRENGTH

By showing up to spend time with God every day and by using His promptings to overcome my self-limiting beliefs, I was able to overcome my 35 percent loss in revenue. But that's not all. Thanks to God's provision, I was able to finish 2020 *having earned more in one year than I'd earned during any year of my life*, including when I'd been President of Sales for a national contractor.

Even more important than that financial win, I was able to finish 2020 stronger spiritually and relationally than I had 2019. I was closer to God than I had ever been, and I had experienced more peace during the wild ups and downs of the year than I normally feel when I think I am in control. I was also stronger relationally, and even though 2020 was a challenging year for everyone in our family, we were able to grow closer to one another along the way as we discussed much of the content you'll find in these pages.

Then, over the course of 2021, the verses and the applications in this book were battle tested as I referred to them again and again on my difficult days. I also shared them with executive coaching clients and watched them experience success as well! In fact, over the course of this past year, I have shared this information with sixty business leaders, either in one-on-one or group coaching engagements. This number does not include the many people who attended one of my workshops or speaking events where these topics were addressed, or the readers of my weekly leadership emails, or my "Win at Home First" podcast listeners.

These sixty business leaders spoke with me from the other end of a phone call or video conference call, or from right across a table. These individuals are all leading teams and families, just like you.

They have bad days, just like you. They have arguments with their spouse, feel anger toward their kids, are nervous about meeting their annual financial goals, and experience decision fatigue related to masks, vaccines, working from home, and more.

These leaders include CEOs, regional managers, CFOs, account managers, business owners, sales leaders, and sourcing managers, just to name a few of their roles. They come from a wide range of industries, including wealth management, construction, marketing, service industries, medical, and consumer goods. These are people who have jobs similar to yours, who have similar demands on their time, and who face very similar problems. The content in this book helped them to overcome feelings of defeat and discouragement, and it helped set them up to experience wins each day. I am confident that it will do the same for *you*.

I don't promise that this book will guarantee you experience a financial bump. What I'm presenting is not prosperity gospel. However, I do believe that if you are disciplined each day in your pursuit of God, and if you show up consistently to serve others, you will see success in various areas of your life. Matthew 6:33 says, "But seek first the kingdom of God and his righteousness, and all these things will be added to you."

My prayer for you is that after reading this book, you will feel stronger and more excited and encouraged to go after all that God has in store for you. Regardless of what battle you are currently facing, this content can help equip you to overcome the stresses of the day, grow closer to God, and win the day!

It is time to rise and go!

3

WHAT DOES "RISE AND GO" MEAN?

How To Get The Most Out Of This Book

In Acts 8–10 in the English Standard Version, God tells three different people to "rise and go," and that phrase and the people's responses stood out to me during this time in my life. First, in Acts 8:26, God tells Philip through an angel to "rise and go" to meet with the Ethiopian eunuch. Then in Acts 9:11, God tells Ananias through a vison to "rise and go" to meet with Saul, which is part of the incredible story of Saul's conversion and transformation to becoming Paul. Finally, in Acts 10:20, the Holy Spirit tells Peter to "rise and go" and meet three men who were sent by Cornelius, a centurion and man of power.

In all three incidents, the men involved had no idea what was happening or what would be asked of them when they got to their destination. However, they *did* know that God had given them the command to "rise and go" and had told them the next step. God had only given them one clear next step and not the entire play-by-play, which is the same thing He does for you and me.

What was inspiring to me is that each of these individuals, when they heard from God, was immediately obedient and got up and went where God had said to go.

I pray that I can be that obedient!

UP AND TO THE RIGHT

In my book *Win at Home First*, I shared a graph entitled "Up and to the Right," which illustrates the concept that we want the various areas of our lives—financial growth, new healthy habits (such as going to the gym), etc.—to always show progress indicated by lines that go up and to the right.

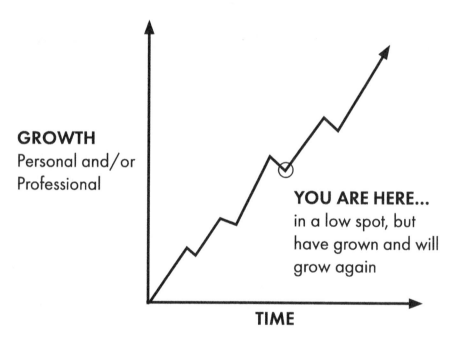

GROWTH
Personal and/or
Professional

YOU ARE HERE...
in a low spot, but
have grown and will
grow again

TIME

If you "zoom in" on any of those graphs, however, you will see that lines that go up and to the right do not do so in a straight manner. Instead, the lines have peaks and valleys as they rise. Let's use numbers as a visual. Say that yesterday's line value was at 40, and today it is at 35. If tomorrow it is at 45, the trend will indeed be "up and to the right." Yet there is still a low spot today at 35.

This low spot is what I am talking about! That is the moment for which I wrote the book.

We all find ourselves in these low spots from time to time. You may refer to those low spots as valleys or ruts. In some Christian circles they're even called "the wilderness," as a reference to the forty days Jesus spent in the wilderness before He started His mission of spreading the Good News. When we are in these low spots, we often feel as though we will be stuck there forever. When we are in a low spot, we can't see our way out, and we don't know where to turn.

Whenever I talk with clients on days when they're feeling discouraged, I draw out this "Up and to the Right" graph. I then circle a low spot, or valley, and tell them that this is where they currently are. I encourage them by showing them the growth they've experienced that has led up to this point in a particular area we are discussing—for example, their business, their marriage, their health, or their quiet time. Once we've reestablished confidence in their earlier growth, I then give them hope that they will grow again. Next, we talk about their current low spot.

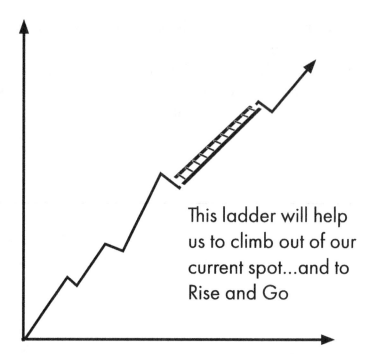

This ladder will help us to climb out of our current spot...and to Rise and Go

First, I draw a ladder that leads from the bottom of the graph's valley, which I have already circled, to the top of the next peak. We then talk about the need for them to establish ladder rungs that will help them climb out of the valley so that they can "rise and go."

Next, I share tools and resources to help my client build their ladder rungs. Those tools and resources are in this book, ready to help you!

THE STEPS TO RISE AND GO

The ladder and the ladder rungs are our response to God's call for each of us to "rise and go." God does not want us to sit and wallow in our sadness or insecurity. God does not want us to be discouraged after an argument with a spouse or a bad financial month at the office. God wants us to *get up and go*. He doesn't want us to remain defeated, discouraged, or scared. God wants us to move each and every day toward expanding the Kingdom.

This book provides the tools to help you do just that. The rest of the book is organized in two parts. The first part is "Rise." We all get knocked down from time to time, and this section provides tools to help us build the courage to get back up and reestablish our footing. These chapters will help you reinstate your hope and faith for what you have been building up to this point and will get you ready to start climbing up your ladder that leads out of the valley. In this section, we will cover ten key topics: desires, gratitude, positivity, faith, hope, intentionality, strengths, courage, rejection, and provision.

The next part of the book is "Go." These chapters will help you build confidence so you can start climbing the ladder and taking steps that lead "up and to the right" on the graph. In this section, we will focus on goals, mindset, preparedness, peace, commitment, obedience, encouragement, perseverance, consistency, and celebration.

This adds up to twenty chapters in parts 2 and 3. Each chapter includes:

- a thought-provoking question related to the chapter's key topic
- one leadership trait related to that topic
- a related Bible verse
- a devotional reading that draws on stories from business leaders and my personal experiences
- action steps for your personal implementation
- a prayer to help you process the content and move forward in your life

I encourage you to have a pen and paper at the ready, or an electronic writing device, so you can take notes as you read. When people are engaged in writing information down, we tend to be more focused. When we just think about the information instead, we frequently find that thirty seconds later we have moved on from the exercise and are thinking about something else. As a result, we don't experience any real change.

When we take the time to slow down and read content care-fully, we can begin to think about how it applies to our own life. We may even hear from God. I encourage you to commit to reading a single chapter each day and spending five to ten minutes with it. Some chapters may include content that resonates deeply with you, so take more time with those. The time you spend with God will help you reflect, and the prayer you offer up will help you discern how this content applies to your life.

Since there are twenty chapters for "Rise" and "Go," you can use this book as a monthly devotional guide: starting a new chapter each workday over a period of four weeks. However, a few chap-ters may speak to you more than others. So I encourage you to go deeper with those readings that resonate. I had to reflect on some of these ideas and verses for a few days, and even weeks, and you may want to do so as well.

QR codes were added throughout this book to improve your experience with the book's content. Some QR codes will lead you to podcast episodes that coincide with the chapter to provide addi-tional information on a particular business leader or the podcast topic. Other QR codes, such as the one on this page and on the back of the book, take you to the *Rise and Go* landing page, www.cory-mcarlson.com/riseandgo. This webpage has additional resources that were thoughtfully provided with you in mind and will include future feedback from readers like you.

Scan the QR code to find additional Rise and Go resources

RISE AND GO MANIFESTO

Over the last couple of years, I've created a manifesto document that I review a few mornings every week. I've found that by using this as a ladder rung, it helps to elevate my mindset. Reading this manifesto helps me shake off the doubts and insecurities that I wake up with occasionally. It reminds me of how far God has brought me and of the truth that He will not abandon me now.

Throughout this book, I will provide guidance that you can use to help create your own Rise and Go Manifesto. I encourage you to create a Google document or Word file in which to store this information. You can see a template at www.corymcarlson.com/riseandgo. I've also provided in the back of this book a description of each of the sections I include in my personal Rise and Go Manifesto.

To this day, I still receive notes from past clients that detail how these tools and this document have helped them and still help them, even though we no longer work together. Here is one recent note from Jim Barter, an executive in the medical industry:

> One of the many coaching tips you provided was the idea of pulling together a Reframing Mindset document. My recollection of our conversation is that you said it would be good to have and pull out to help remind me of who I am, where I came from, and where I'm headed and that such a document was key to have on my down days.
>
> While thankfully I've not had too many, today was one of those post-holiday, dreary days when I needed to get back in the saddle and was just not feeling it.
>
> I pulled out my Reframing Document. It really helped me to refresh and renew.
>
> So thanks on several fronts.

My prayer is that this document helps you as well, just as it has helped Jim.

Now it's time to rise and go!

PART 2

RISE

Build the Courage
to Get Back Up

4

WHAT DO YOU WANT?

Leadership Trait: Desires

John 1:38, "Jesus turned and saw them following and said to them, 'What are you seeking?'"

The first of Jesus's words reported in the book of John do not take the form of a statement. Jesus's first words in John are actually a question.

We know that Jesus was a great teacher, but we don't always recognize the significance of questions in His teachings. A quick Google search reveals that in the Bible, Jesus was asked 183 questions. In contrast, He asked 307 questions of others. Asking questions was a big part of Jesus's style of teaching and of the way He had conversations!

I think He asked questions for several reasons.

First, He was interested in learning the audience's perspective. Once He knew this, He could customize His message to show how the Good News could meet their specific needs. The root of His message was always the same. But the context varied, depending on His audience and their desires.

To the woman at the well, He talked about "living water." To the disciples trying to catch fish, He talked about "catching men." Jesus always speaks to His listeners in a language that they understand.

Another important reason Jesus asked questions was because when people answered, this allowed them to verbalize what they wanted. There is power in saying what one wants out loud. Science backs this up.

Clinical psychologist Carla Marie Manly, Ph.D., says that "speaking out loud to oneself allows us to sort through our thoughts in a more conscious manner." Put another way, when we say things out loud, we become more aware of what is going on in our mind. Manly goes on to say, "we become more conscious of the mind's ramblings and can then become more intentional."[2]

A 2011 study published in the *Quarterly Journal of Experimental Psychology* reported on the potential benefits of talking to oneself. In this study, twenty participants were instructed to locate certain objects in a grocery store. In the first trial, no one was allowed to talk out loud as they searched for the items. In the second trial, the participants were instructed to repeat the names of the objects out loud as they searched for them. All of the participants found the items more quickly in the second trial![3]

Speaking words out loud helps us to focus on what we are searching for. Saying "mustard" numerous times, for example, will

---

2   Carla Marie Manly, quoted by Georgina Berbari, "Talking to Yourself Is Normal. Here's When You Should Be Concerned," October 18, 2020, https://www.considerable.com/health/symptoms-health/is-it-normal-to-talk-to-yourself-keep-it-up-according-to-science/.

3   Gary Lupyan and Daniel Swingley, "Self-Directed Speech Affects Visual Search Performance," *The Quarterly Journal of Experimental Psychology*, April 11, 2011, https://www.tandfonline.com/doi/abs/10.1080/17470218.2011.647039?journalCode=pqje20#preview.

help you stay focused on finding the mustard, so that you don't get distracted by all the other items on the shelves that are just waiting to grab your attention.

HOW WILL YOU ANSWER?

Whenever a paralyzed man or a blind man approached Jesus, He would ask the man a key question: "What do you want?" To most of us, that seems like a silly question. We think: Wouldn't anyone who was paralyzed want to be able to walk? Didn't all blind people want to be able to regain their sight?

That may be the case. But Jesus still asks the questions. As a result, each person had to say what they truly wanted out loud.

So what about you? What do *you* want?

Seriously, what do you want?

If Jesus were to walk right into your office, your house, or wherever you are at right now and ask, "What do you want?" what would be your answer?

Do you want the next quarter in your business to be a strong one? Do you desire an improved relationship with your teenager? To overcome an addiction? To obtain financial freedom? To launch your own business? To find a spouse—or, if you're already married, to improve your relationship?

When I'm working with clients, I use an exercise in which I ask them what they want. In it, I ask a few questions, such as, "What would success in this area look like in six months?" "If we were to celebrate in one year with a bottle of champagne, what would we be celebrating?" "What do you want to see happen within one year—or three, or five?" I ask for answers that address both the personal and professional areas of their life.

I do this exercise for a couple reasons. First, the process requires them to slow down and think about what they actually want. So often in life, we focus on accomplishing tasks, yet we have forgotten why we are even doing them. It's important to ask: *What are all my efforts for? What is the big picture? Where am I headed?*

The other reason I do it is that once I know what they want, then I know where I can help and how I can add value to their lives. I am then able to customize my coaching program to hold them accountable for reaching their stated goals. I can help them to stay focused on what they want and not become distracted or go off track.

As you consider these questions, you may find it very difficult to answer them. The first time I tried, I came up blank, and so do many of my clients. But why is it so hard for us to answer these questions?

It's unlikely that anybody ever specifically told us not to answer these types of questions. Yet I think many of us internalized the idea that we shouldn't. We feel that if we focus too much on what we want, then we are being selfish and not thinking of others. So when we try to consider these questions, we experience feelings of guilt.

There are also some of us who don't like to answer this question, or to pray about what we desire, because we don't like the thought of treating God like a genie. But that is not what I'm proposing. I'm not advising that anyone treat God as some kind of ATM or Santa Claus. However, God *does* want us to go after something. God wants us to find something in life to pursue that will expand the Kingdom and bring Glory to Him, while also bringing us joy. Psalm 37:4 says, "Delight yourself in the Lord, and He will give you the desires of your heart."

One thing I love about parenting is that it sometimes leads to moments when I get a glimpse of how God feels about us. One example of this has to do with my son Kaleb, who is nine years old and a very good athlete for his age. Up until now, he has only played recreational sports, and we have not yet signed him up for any of the competitive youth sports teams that are commonplace today. However, soon he will have to decide if he wants to play soccer, basketball, or football year-round.

Regardless of his choice, I am going to support him in his decision. As a dad, I just want him to pick the sport that he enjoys the most, try his hardest, have fun, and be the light to his teammates—and in the process, bring glory to God.

God is the same way. He does not mind how we answer the question of what we want. He just wants us to pursue with excellence the desires that align with His heart, and so to bring Him glory.

So, what do you want?

Keep in mind that you are not answering this question for life. You don't need to have a perfect answer that will look great on your tombstone someday. You only need to answer the question for right now. Where do you need God's help in your life? Where are you wanting God to provide some favor?

Whether your answer applies just to today or to a longer period of time, you need to start taking the actions necessary to make that desire a reality. You need to move toward that situation, relationship, or opportunity with both feet, pursue it with excellence, and bring glory to God in the process.

"TO PAINT AGAIN"

One of my favorite client stories is of a time when I worked with a business leader named Kyle. Earlier in his career, Kyle had been very creative as a designer and illustrator. But due to the busyness of life, he had put his creative endeavors aside, especially painting.

When I asked him the question, "What do you want?" he slowly responded with the words: "To paint again." The slowness of his response came out of guilt he felt because he'd been led to believe that an answer like that was selfish. Shouldn't his answer involve his wife and daughter? Shouldn't his response have something to do with leadership, work, or serving others?

My response surprised him. I told him that painting was not selfish and that pursuing the creative practice of painting could in fact make him a better leader, father, and husband. Art would connect him to God, give him rest, utilize his creativity, and fill his heart up so he could be better in all areas of his life. Making art was not selfish!

I encouraged him to make his desire a reality. I told him to start pulling this dream forward into the present, instead of pushing it out into the black hole of the future. Over the next few weeks of coaching calls, we discussed steps he could take each day. Over those weeks, he began to check items off the list. These included gathering his paint, purchasing canvases, and renting a studio. Most importantly, he started to paint.

One day I received a surprise package on my front door. I was stunned to see what was inside. Kyle had made a painting that was incredible and looked like something from a gallery! To be honest, I'd had no idea Kyle was such a good painter! I felt especially touched by the concept of the painting. The image was of a four-person tandem red bike against a yellow background. The four-person bike represented the group coaching call I led every other week with Kyle and two other clients.

The painting still hangs above my fireplace, not only because it is beautiful, but also because it's an inspiring reminder that God wants us to answer the question, "What do we want?" and then boldly go after the subject of our answer.

ACTION STEPS

Spend ten minutes listing all that you want for your business and life: today, this week, and this month. This part is critical, as reestablishing one's footing is a key step in starting to dream again!

Next, spend five minutes in prayer to see if you get clarity about which of these desires to pursue first. Start a list of action steps you can take that will get you one step closer to your dreams.

In the weeks ahead, keep an eye out for opportunities to act on these steps. Or choose one or two steps that you already know you can take, and schedule time in your calendar now to do them.

BONUS: RISE AND GO MANIFESTO

Some of the items that you list can be added to the "What I want" section of your Rise and Go Manifesto. In my own manifesto,

I have added pictures and a one- to two-sentence description of each desire I've listed for both my personal life and professional life.

One personal example is that I want to go on a mission trip with each of my kids. I have already been to Nicaragua with Kiley, my oldest, but I also want to go on mission trips with Kamdyn and Kaleb at some point in the future. A professional example is that I want to host a large leadership event for business leaders in Cincinnati.

You can choose whatever you like. Try to identify goals for both your personal life and your professional life.

PRAYER

Lord, when I read this chapter and consider the question "What do you want?" my mind just races. What if I choose the wrong thing? What if I pick something you don't want me to do? When I feel unsure, please help me remember that you have given me freedom of choice and that, by opening and closing doors, you'll help redirect my course as I move forward. Amen.

5

WHAT ARE YOUR WINS?

Leadership Trait: Gratitude

Genesis 1:12, "The earth brought forth vegetation, plants yielding seed according to their own kinds, and trees bearing fruit in which is their seed, each according to its kind. And God saw that it was good."

The devil knows that one of the easiest ways to knock down a hard-charging and driven individual is to get that person to look at what is unfinished! He wants us to focus our attention on what is just getting started or in that messy middle phase, and not on what we have already done; what is messy and in progress versus what is clean and complete. Why? Because the devil knows that we will feel discontented and discouraged if we keep our eyes on the mess instead of noticing our progress and success.

Last year I took my daughter Kiley, then sixteen, with me to Pawleys Island, South Carolina, for a leadership summit. On the first night of the three-day event, participants broke off into pairs and did a reflection exercise that involved answering specific questions. Kiley and I both spent individual quiet time writing down our answers to these questions.

After a while, we came back together to share what each of us had written down. She went first and, as you would expect from any father, I felt very proud and even teared up while hearing what she had written down.

Then it was my turn.

I read through all my answers. When I was done, I expected to see her looking impressed by everything I'd said. Impressed by all the wisdom I had as an adult and an executive coach, in contrast to what she knew as a teenager and a student.

Well, that was not the case!

When I got done reading my answers, I looked up and said, "Well, what do you think?"

She quickly said, "Dad, you sound angry."

"What? What do you mean I sound angry?"

As we discussed what she'd observed, it became clear that while I had a few achievements written down, most of what was written down was my unfinished work. I had already forgotten about progress and was focused on what was not yet done. My daughter could hear it in the tone of my voice as I shared what I'd written down.

Yes, I'd just had the best quarter of my business, but what about the next quarter?

I already had speaking engagements scheduled, but how was I going to get more of them?

Sure, I'd just finalized a contract for my book to be published in another country. But how was I going to get published in more countries?

What about all the courses I had yet to build and the live events I still needed to plan and host? What about the additional books I wanted to write?

Can you relate?

How content are you with the present? Have you, like me, forgotten your accomplishments because you are so busy looking at what you have left to finish?

God's mindset in Genesis offers a refreshing reminder of what our emotional posture needs to be. As He was creating the world over six days, He paused at the end of each one and "saw that it was good."

The Scripture doesn't say that God was disappointed He had only gotten so much done. At the end of day two, God doesn't say, "Oh, man, I only created the land and water. I didn't do anything with vegetation, plus I still have to create all the animals."

No, He took pleasure in what He had already made. He ended each day with gratitude and contentment over what He had created, not discontentment over what He had not yet created.

In an article posted on June 7, 2008, titled "Goal Progress and Happiness" on *Psychology Today's* website, Timothy Pychyl, Ph.D., said, "The research on goal pursuit and well-being reveals an interesting cycle between progress on our goals and our reports of happiness and life satisfaction." His summary of his research is simple, yet profound: "Progress on our goals makes us happier and more satisfied with life."[4]

The meaning of this is also simple: We need to end each day with gratitude over what we've done instead of looking at all the unchecked boxes on our to-do list.

Yes, we need to have a plan that gets us where we are headed and addresses the items we have yet to complete. Yes, we need to

---

4   Timothy Pychyl, "Goal Progress and Happiness," *Psychology Today*, June 7, 2008, https://www.psychologytoday.com/us/blog/dont-delay/200806/goal-progress-and-happiness.

have a vision for where we want our businesses to be. However, a road map is a tool to help us get where we are headed, not a measuring stick to beat ourselves up with each day.

Too often we focus on what we have not accomplished instead of celebrating what we have completed. This may be out of greed for more or envy of others. Either way, a focus on what has yet to be accomplished leads to a lack of motivation and confidence. When this happens, we stop making progress toward our goals.

In an article titled "Confidence Matters for Athletes," Sports Psychologist Dr. Jim Taylor wrote, "If you have low confidence, you can't help but focus on all of the negative things rather than on things that will enable you to perform your best. All of this accumulated negativity hurts your motivation."[5]

This is probably why God wants us to celebrate wins. We can see this in the Parable of the Talents. When the master returns and learns that two of his three servants have doubled their investment, he says, "Let's celebrate together" (Matthew 25:23 NLT).

You might be thinking that you need to keep building your business and that no one can sit around celebrating all the time. It's a good point. However, celebration *is* a necessary mindset shift. If we want to be motivated, we need to have the posture of gratitude for progress, not one of discontent over what has yet to be completed.

GRATITUDE IS POWER

We can use gratitude as a weapon against discontent, boredom, and complacency in our lives. There are also emotional and physical benefits to experiencing gratitude in our lives—benefits that can manifest as an increase in dopamine, an improved immune system, better energy, or improved mental health. It is well known that a person can't be stressed and smiling at the same time!

All this became clear to me at the conference I attended with Kiley. In fact, that experience with my daughter really rocked my

---

5   Jim Taylor, "Confidence Matters for Athletes," HuffPost, May 25, 2011, https://www.huffpost.com/entry/confidence-matters-for-at_b_827666.

world. I knew that if my sixteen-year-old daughter's impression of my year-to-date reflections was "You sound angry," then something had to be wrong with my mindset.

I wondered, *What kind of example am I to her if she only sees my discontent?* She had seen that I had my eyes only on the chase and that I was focused on the pursuit of more money and more business! I knew I needed to change my mindset. And so, as soon as we returned from that trip, I started writing down three things I am grateful for each day.

At the time of this writing, I have been consistently writing down my top three wins for each day for over a year and a half. In fact, I've probably done this on 90 percent of those days! Although I still have emotionally low days, like we all do, I am definitely more motivated and optimistic than I was before I started this routine. The impact this one small action has had in my life is so enormous, in fact, that I now encourage everyone to do it.

Over the last year, I have started each of my coaching calls by asking my client, "What is one personal win and one professional win you had in the last week?" Often, newer clients have to stop and think about it. They might even say, "I don't know if I had a win."

Clients I have been working with for a while, however, expect the question, so they are prepared. In fact, they usually have a few wins to pick from. That's because they've experienced a mindset shift, and so now they are aware of their wins.

Even on our worst weeks, we all have wins. It might be a great conversation, the continuation of a strong habit, or a trip to the gym. The fact that we struggle to remember this illuminates the fact that we're often focused on the negative or what is not yet completed.

Focusing on the wins in my own life creates momentum. Getting my clients to focus on their own wins creates momentum for them too. When we focus on our wins, we all start to view our days as God viewed His six days of creation: "it was good."

ACTION STEPS

Take five minutes to write down three professional wins and three personal wins from the last week.

Starting tonight, I also want you to write down three wins (or three things you are grateful for) from the day. Do this every night, moving forward. Alternatively, you could write down three wins from the previous day, starting tomorrow, and continue this practice every morning.

BONUS

If you want to do an exercise similar to the one Kiley and I did at the leadership retreat, you can answer these questions:

- What is the fruit you are currently experiencing in your life?
- What are the frustrations you are currently facing?
- What are your future dreams you are praying for?
- What are some failures you are carrying with you?

Once you write down your answers, write down some action steps you can take to help move some of your frustrations, future dreams, and perceived failures towards being a fruitful area of your life.

PRAYER

Lord, thank you for all that you have given me. I want to notice how you are helping me grow each day as an individual, a parent, a spouse, a friend, and a business leader. Help me to enjoy the process and to not be so focused on the finish line, which is always so elusive! Amen.

6

WHAT GOOD WILL COME OF THIS?

Leadership Trait: Positivity

Romans 8:28, "And we know that for those who love God all things work together for good, for those who are called according to his purpose."

"Cory, I thought you were Mr. Positive."

It still stings a little bit when I replay this memory in my mind. A little over a year ago, a group of men from a community small group were working on a volunteer service project, pulling weeds and removing brush from a running path.

This was during the COVID pandemic and a few weeks before the 2020 presidential election, so there were many topics running through people's minds. At one moment in the day, as we were talking—or, more accurately, complaining—about COVID, we began to discuss the inconsistencies we seemed to be experiencing with everything, such as how people were responding differently to the crisis, how companies' quarantine requirements differed, and contradictions in news reporting and mask requirements, not only in different parts of the country but even in different parts of our own city.

While we were talking, one of my buddies said in surprise, "Cory, I thought you were Mr. Positive."

We all laughed at his comment. I may have even pushed back a little at the time. And then the conversation moved on.

However, a few days later during my quiet time, it really hit me.

I *had* always been Mr. Positive before. I even won the "Inspirational Award" on the high school soccer team my senior year because of my positivity. But that morning, I realized that instead of keeping a positive outlook on life no matter the circumstances, as I had in the past, I was now allowing my circumstances to define my happiness and my outlook on life: politics, COVID, quarantine, business ups and downs, virtual schooling, friends losing jobs, clients stressed out, live events—such as church—getting cancelled . . . the list goes on and on.

That day, I happened to be reading Romans, and when I got to Romans 8:28 I was reminded that for those who love God, all things work together for good. The verse doesn't just say that God uses things for *better*, and it doesn't say that God uses just *some* things in this way. No, it promises that God uses *all* things for *good*. Even our bad circumstances. Even the bad parts of these last couple of years.

As I reflected on this verse, I started to see some good that had come out of recent events. On a personal level, the quarantine had allowed us to spend a lot more time together as a family, as dance, gymnastics, and other events were reduced or cancelled. We played board games, built puzzles, watched movies, and walked to the coffee shop. I threw the football with my son. These were all fun events that we used to do occasionally. Recently, we'd been able to do them daily. Also, as travel started to open back up in the summer of 2020, we were able to take some great trips. This included a family vacation to Missouri, the previously mentioned father/daughter trip to Pawleys Island, South Carolina, and a few college visits.

Such benefits weren't just limited to my family. I wasn't the only one whose calendar was freed up during this time due to cancelled travel. As a result, my friends and I were able to meet up for a coffee or beer more frequently than we had prior to COVID.

I even had time to strategize ways I could help more leaders with my business. Choosing to invest in myself, I participated in a new coaching program that required participants to spend a lot of time watching videos, participating in coaching calls, and executing new ideas. I also launched my podcast, "Win at Home First," in April 2020.

I probably would not have made these investments if it were not for the slowdown. But because I did make them, I was able to come alongside clients as they made incredible breakthroughs, even while wrestling with challenges related to their businesses, working from home, and their children's virtual schools, on top of all the other stress they were experiencing.

Though it's easier said than done, we all need to remember this verse as we are building our businesses and our lives. As we run into roadblocks and disappointments, we must put our hope in God's promise and not in our circumstances.

Yes, my friend's "Mr. Positive" comment stung a little. However, I am grateful now, because I needed that "slap in the face" to remind me of where I want to put my hope.

HOW CAN WE TURN THIS TO GOOD?

When I think about commitment to a positive mindset, I think of Nic Manning, who is co-owner of a multimillion-dollar construction company, Manning Contracting. One day, Nic's team discovered that an employee had made a $250,000 mistake on a construction job! Yes, a $250,000 mistake, not a small $25 mistake. This mistake was not something they could ask the client to pay for. Instead, the loss would have to come out of the company's own pocket.

Some leaders would have stormed off and fired the employee. But Nic didn't. Now, don't get me wrong: firing team members is sometimes the right thing to do, and God is not a fan of people doing sloppy work. However, Nic knew that this mistake was uncharacteristic for this individual, so he was trying to find the good in this situation.

With this in mind, he led his team through the exercise of asking how they could turn this situation into good. After the brainstorming session, the company put into place some new processes to make sure such a mistake would not happen again. They also identified a few new opportunities for improving the bidding process for future construction projects.

Nic was able to take a bad situation, see it from God's perspective, and think through how to turn this unfortunate situation into something good.

One benefit of spending more time in the Word and growing closer to God is that you start to see things the way God does. Of course, God is all-knowing, and that is something we can never be. However, we need to work toward aligning our hearts with His, turning toward Him one degree at a time.

When we start to align our heart with God, we can start to see that He is, indeed, using all things for good. We start to see more of the good in our lives, not just the bad. In contrast, when we are focused on our own ways, then we tend to be controlled by our circumstances. I think of this as an attempt to do life without God.

However, God does not want us to do life *without Him* or *for Him*. God wants us to do it *with Him*. He made people to enjoy a relationship with Him. We see this in Genesis 3:8, when He is in the Garden of Eden looking for Adam and Eve "in the cool of the day." As Skye Jethani writes on the back cover of his book, *With*: "Stop living your life under, over, from, and for God and start living in communion with Him."[6]

---

6   Skye Jethani, *With: Reimagining the Way You Relate to God* (Nashville: Thomas Nelson, 2011).

God wants us all to help Him expand His Kingdom. However, we need to swallow our pride to realize God does not *need* us. God has been at work since the beginning of time and will continue until the end of time.

It is humbling to say this, but we are just a blip on the radar. Just a speck of sand at the beach. Truth be told, we can only do so much in this world by ourselves. I can only send out so many messages, make so many connections, and perform so many other tasks to grow my business and impact people. It takes the help of God, though, to really get things moving.

"LET'S GO WHERE HE IS MOVING"

Scan QR code to listen to the podcast

William and Kristen Schumacher are a married couple and founders of Uprising Food, a company that makes healthy food and chips. I first got to know them when they were guests on my podcast. But I got to know them even better when the two of them participated in my "Confident and Consistent Leader" challenge in early 2022. This is a thirty-day challenge that is available to all business leaders that I run every few months. During these thirty days, leaders receive daily emails with teachings, as well as weekly coaching calls, to help them grow in confidence in their leadership and consistency in their habits. More information can be found at www.corymcarlson.com/leadership.

Scan QR code to learn more about the challenge

One day during the challenge, they had an important business meeting that was cancelled. Instead of allowing the cancellation to ruin their day, or maybe even a few of their days, Kristen typed into the challenge's group chat, "I watched in awe of my husband's leadership for our family and our business as he himself was able to still see a win and said, 'God just isn't moving there. Let's go where He's moving.'"

As you go forward today, lean into doing life *with* God and consider how you can keep from being derailed when things do not go your way. Whether you're facing a bad month in business, a difficult relationship, bad health news, or a cancelled meeting, ask yourself how you can trust and pray for God to use these situations for good.

This awareness will elevate your mindset so that you can use the experiences of today for good tomorrow.

ACTION STEPS

Spend five minutes listing the items that you are perceiving as bad today, both in your business and your personal life. What are the challenges you are facing?

Now, spend five minutes listing the good that has already come from those situations, and write down your ideas about the good that may yet come from it.

PRAYER

Lord, this one is hard for me. Sometimes I don't take the time to lift my head up out of the sand and try to see the bigger picture. However, time and time again, you bring good out of bad things in my life. So, Lord, I pray that I will learn to use the bad in my life for good, as you have modeled. Thank you for working all things for good. Amen.

7

WHO HAS THE NIGHTSHIFT?

Leadership Trait: Faith

Psalm 127:1–2, "Unless the Lord builds the house, those who build it labor in vain. Unless the Lord watches over the city, the watchman stays awake in vain. It is in vain that you rise up early and go late to rest, eating the bread of anxious toil; for he gives to his beloved sleep."

One consistent area of weakness for me is that I tend to have the sense that I am in control. There are times when I believe there is a direct correlation between my efforts and how my business and life go. I trust that the more emails I send, the more social media posts I make, and the more coffee and lunches I have with prospects, the more my businesses will grow.

You may feel the same way. Many of my clients do.

When we believe that our efforts are responsible for the growth of our businesses, then we also believe that when we are not working, nothing positive is happening on that front. In other words, we tend to think that if we don't work, our business won't grow. And so we never stop working. However, that belief is not true. The verses from Psalm 127 remind me to trust that the success in my business and life does not all fall on me.

Maybe these verses will help you as well.

As the verses promise, God is also at work on our behalf. When it comes to our lives and our businesses, God has the nightshift! He is working behind the scenes, even as you read this book.

While we are doing outreach and holding business development meetings, God is softening the hearts of prospects who will in time work with us. Even better, while we are sleeping, spending time with our families, or having fun with friends, God is also at work on our behalf, in both our personal and professional lives.

Great leaders believe this verse to be true. That is why they can set boundaries and honor them.

Scan QR code to listen to the podcast

One day on my podcast, Jordan Raynor, one of my favorite Christian business authors, shared with me that he stops working at 5 p.m. every day. Yes, there are those rare times he must work after the kids go to bed or on the weekends, due to a deadline. However, a majority of the time, Jordan stops at 5 p.m. so he can be with his family.

How can he do this when he has a goal of selling one million books by the end of 2025? Because Jordan trusts that God has the nightshift!

When we don't believe God has the nightshift, then we are constantly looking at our devices to make sure we don't lose out on any opportunity. We constantly check our email to make sure we don't have to answer any questions from a customer, because we fear that we will lose them if we don't respond immediately.

We check our social media to see if we have a note waiting for us from a prospect who wants to do business with us. Or maybe, we think, a potential client commented on our post. We think that if we do not respond immediately, then we will lose the prospect or customer.

According to global tech care company Asurion, Americans check their phones on average ninety-six times a day.[7] That breaks down to once every ten minutes! Of course, those numbers include the times we go to the phone due to social media addictions and the dopamine hit we get just by looking at our phone. But for myself and for many others, a lot of those times can be blamed on a fear of loss.

Scan QR code to listen to the podcast

Jason Lippert is CEO of LCI, a four and a half billion dollar annual revenue global company with more than 15,000 employees and listed on the New York Stock Exchange. During my podcast interview with him, he stunned me when he said that he does not

---

7   Asurion-sponsored survey by Market Research Firm Solidea Solutions conducted August 18–20, 2019, of 1,998 U.S. smartphone users, compared to an Asurion-sponsored survey conducted by market research company OnePoll between Sept. 11–19, 2017, of 2,000 U.S. adults with a smartphone.

take his computer home at night. Our inner naysayers will react, "Well, of course *he* doesn't need his laptop with him. He has a strong team around him!" However, we all know that there are CEOs of both bigger and smaller companies who are surrounded by great teams but don't know when to stop working.

Over the last few years of working with clients, this is one of the more common challenges I've seen executive leaders face. They struggle with knowing when to stop working and with keeping their boundaries related to work and rest, because they feel the company's success all depends on them.

When I am working with clients who are facing this challenge, I share a few truths to help change their mindset. The first is the fact that work is never-ending. It is infinite and we will never catch up. Author Simon Sinek talks about this in his best-selling book *The Infinite Game*. Sports are a finite game, where there is a winner and a loser. There is a first play and last play of the game. A first game of the season and last game of the season. Business, on the other hand, is never-ending. Each day builds on the previous day. Each quarter builds on the previous quarter. This is why we must behave as if we are running a marathon and not a sprint. We need to adjust our efforts for the long game. Yes, there are times when we must work late. But we need to manage our energy if our efforts are to be sustainable.

When we accept the infinite mindset, we acknowledge we will never keep up with all the emails we receive. We agree that there are endless possibilities for outreach. Basically, we must confront the brutal fact that we will never catch up with all the work there is to be done!

The second truth I tell my clients is that their business is not dependent on them personally. I help them realize this by looking backwards. We look at some of the employees they have recently hired, or projects they have won, or new connections they have made. During that conversation, the leader starts to see that they were not involved in 100 percent of the process.

YOU ARE NOT 100% IN CONTROL, AND THAT'S A GOOD THING

One client of mine, Brayton Deal, owns Iron House Studios, and a while back, his video production company needed a new employee to help oversee much of the production. Hiring this employee would allow Brayton to step more fully into the CEO role and be involved less in the day-to-day tasks involved in video production.

Brayton, as many of us, had self-limiting beliefs that there would not be anybody out there who would be interested in joining his small company. He was feeling the pressure that the company was all dependent on him. To his surprise, however, almost 70 people applied for the job, and after interviewing the top candidates, he was able to land a key hire with a lot of talent and experience coming from a much larger company! Brayton was stunned by this result! I used this scenario to point out that although Brayton had exerted some control by posting a job opening, it was God who had brought the right person, at the right time, to his company.

We are not alone in growing our businesses. As my clients begin to see the many ways that God has been at work with their people and projects in the past, they start to have more faith that He will do it again in the future. When they see that business is infinite, and that the success they enjoy today is not their own doing, they begin to accept that God really does have the nightshift.

We must believe that God is at work on our businesses and our lives, both when we are working and when we are not. God is helping us by day and by night.

Scan QR code to listen to the podcast

Rick Stephens founded Horizon Hobby, a remote-control hobby company, out of his basement and grew it to 330 million dollars in annual revenue. Rick was very vulnerable in a conversation he had with me on my podcast, as he was in his book, *In Plane Sight.* In it, he discussed the depression he'd battled his whole life, which took a significant turn for the better on his forty-fourth birthday.

On that pivotal day, he was sitting in his office chair, as he had numerous times in his life. At the time, his family was in Colorado on a family vacation that he'd chosen to skip out of because of his fear that the business would suffer if he took any time off.

Numerous times throughout his career, Rick had spent hours or even days focused on the fear of whether the future would pan out for the business. *Are we going to keep growing and keep all these people employed? Will the remote-control toy market continue to grow or suddenly dry up? Am I making the right decisions as a leader? Am I helping my team members grow?*

Rick had feared the future many times, and God had helped him many times. But each time, he seemed to forget how God had helped him before. This time, however, Rick had an encounter with God like he never had before. That encounter filled him with a sense of peace. He felt newly convinced that God had gotten him and his business this far and would continue to be involved in Rick's life and business. At that moment, Rick realized that he had spent the first forty-four years of his life depressed, ruminating about the past, or worrying about the future, but never living in the present.

Rick decided that he would not live another forty-four years in this mental state. From that moment on, he was going to live in the moment and have faith that God would provide and help him navigate the future properly.

When we start to believe that God has the nightshift, then we can stop working in order to be with our families—whether on a vacation or just hanging out in the family room at night. This mindset allows us to step away from our phones and email, because we know that we don't have to respond immediately to any notifications. We can go to the gym and work out, rest and read a book, and even play with our kids, knowing that we do not have to work around the clock. We can do this because we know who is really in charge, and thankfully that Someone is not us! Thank goodness, because if it was truly all up to me, then it would not be to the level it can be when we have God on our side.

ACTION STEPS

Take ten minutes to list some of the following developments that have happened in your business over the past month:

- recent projects that you and your company have won
- new hires you have made
- new clients you have gained
- new relationships that you have developed
- anything else that has contributed to your recent success

Now spend five minutes reviewing this list. If you are like me, you will see that you did not put in 100 percent of the effort that led to these results. In fact, God was at work behind the scenes making things happen. The more we are aware of what God has done in our past, the more confidence we can have that He will also help us in our present and future.

Finally, spend five minutes in prayer acknowledging how God has been at work in your life. Pray that God will help you continue to release control and to hand over your workday worries to Him.

BONUS: RISE AND GO MANIFESTO

The writing you've just done is a great start to the "God has the nightshift" section of your Rise and Go Manifesto. Occasionally reviewing your notes about how God has impacted your business will give you the courage to start the day and give you hope for what's to come.

PRAYER

Lord, thank you for being in business with me. Please forgive me for thinking the responsibility for success is all mine. I pray that I will be more disciplined during the day so I can get my work done, and then be at peace at night, knowing you have the nightshift. Lord, thank you so much that it is not all on me. Amen.

8

HOW DO YOU BELIEVE IT WILL TURN OUT?

Leadership Trait: Hope

Mark 9:23, "And Jesus said to him, 'If you can! All things are possible for one who believes.'"

This verse is so powerful for a couple of reasons. First, there are moments when many of us don't really have faith that *Jesus* can fix or help our situation this time. We wonder if Jesus can really heal a broken relationship, improve a damaged team culture at the office, or increase the success of our business.

Second, even if we do have faith that Jesus can help, many of us don't think that *we* can do our part to fix or help the situation. We wonder if we can continue to show up to improve the broken relationship, demonstrate hope and patience for people on our team, or do what it takes to lead our team at work.

At the point that this verse appears in Mark 9, Jesus had wanted to escape the crowds and have some time to rest and be with His close friends, so He headed off to the mountains for six days with Peter, James, and John. Then, while coming back down the mountain, their group saw that the other disciples were unsuccessfully attempting to cast out a demon from a young boy.

The situation must have been tense, with guys yelling at each other, because Jesus said, "What are you arguing about with them?" (v. 16). The father of the boy said that he brought his child to be healed, but the disciples were not able to heal him (v.18).

Jesus asked a few clarifying questions about the situation, and the man finally said, "But if you can do anything . . ." (v. 22). This is where this verse picks up with Jesus saying, "'If you can'! All things are possible for one who believes." The disciples had been unsuccessful in casting out the demon because they did not yet fully believe. Yes, they had cast out demons before. But they were still unsure of themselves and their power.

You and I are often guilty of this same thing. We have seen Jesus at work time and time again in various areas of our lives. Yet we still wonder if He will show up again. We especially harbor doubts in areas of our lives where we are trying something new.

THE POWER OF VISUALIZATION

One way this plays out in our lives is through visualization. In the lead-up to a situation, our belief about what we think the outcome will be is revealed by how we play out the scenario in our head.

Do we picture our presentation going well or failing? Do we visualize the networking event as a success or a bust? Do we think our revenue will be high or low this month? Do we imagine that the conversation with our spouse will go well or blow up?

What we believe, we often end up becoming. Our thoughts turn into self-fulfilling prophecies. If we believe we will be successful, we often *do* become successful. One reason for this is that we don't quit early, since we believe we can overcome any challenges. On the other hand, if we think we will fail, then often we quit once we start to encounter resistance. We feel that we will fail, so why keep pushing?

Scan QR code to listen to the podcast

Alex Harbin, owner of Iron Sharpens Iron, stated on the "Win at Home First" podcast that we need "to start playing the other movie in our head." What he means is that we are constantly playing a sort of movie in our heads in which an upcoming situation has a bad ending. We need to play the movie that has the successful ending instead.

The other day, my then thirteen-year-old daughter, Kamdyn, and I had a great conversation on just this topic. She is a competitive gymnast and is currently having trouble with her back handspring on the beam.

The gym where she trains holds gymnastics practice five days a week, with the last practice of the week happening on Saturday morning, and the first one on Monday night. We don't have a balance beam at home, and Kamdyn knows that she will have to attempt the back handspring at every practice. So between the end of her practice on Saturday and the beginning of her Monday practice, she spends time visualizing attempts of the back handsprings on the beam.

So when she steps up on the beam that Monday night, she has already visualized her attempts probably 200 times. The question is: Were those visualizations negative or positive? Did she visualize herself falling or landing her handsprings successfully?

If she visualizes 200 unsuccessful back handsprings before she even attempts a real one, then it is going to be hard to make a successful attempt! She will get on the beam, experience low confidence, and start to have doubts. As a result, she won't make the attempt with all her ability. She will not jump as high or bend as much as she is able because she already believes that she will not be successful.

If, on the other hand, she has been visualizing success since her last practice, odds are good that she will have a successful back handspring. She will get on the beam with confidence and stand a little taller. When she goes to jump, she will have more power and force, leading to a successful back handspring.

The same principle is true for you and me. The movies we play in our heads show what we believe on a given matter.

Psycho-Cybernetics by Dr. Maxwell Maltz is a great book about mindset, one that is filled with many great quotes. I particularly appreciate two that reinforce the power of visualization. Henry J. Kaiser, known as the father of American shipbuilding, attributed much of his success to the words, "You can imagine your future."[8] And Matt Furey, President of the Psycho-Cybernetics Foundation, says, "The brain and nervous system are continually leading us in the direction of images we think about consciously."[9] Whether we think positively or negatively about an outcome, all indications seem to be that our thoughts lead to self-fulfilling prophesies.

Even the great NBA player Michael Jordan is known to have visualized game winning shots and even winning championships. In the documentary *Michael Jordan to the Max*, Michael talks about how the power of visualization helped him become a master of the game of basketball.[10]

---

8   Maxwell Maltz, *Psycho-Cybernetics* (New York: TarcherPerigee, 2015), 21.

9   Maltz, *Psycho-Cybernetics*, 13.

10 Michael Jordan, in *Michael Jordan to the Max*, dir. Don Kempf and James D. Stern (Giant Screen Films, 2000).

This information tells us that we need to believe in ourselves. Doing so helps us realize what we want to achieve. But our strength doesn't stop there. As believers, we also benefit from an even greater superpower: the help of Jesus, which is available to us in every situation we navigate. As Jesus says in John 14:12, "Truly, truly, I say to you, whoever believes in me will also do the works that I do; and greater works than these will he do, because I am going to the Father." This is the case whether our aim is to lose weight, deliver a powerful presentation, have a successful month, or land a back handspring on a balance beam.

Just to be clear, all these attempts require proper training and preparation! If you are not a gymnast, don't walk up to a beam, visualize success, and then attempt a back handspring for the first time. The same is true for a work presentation. Don't walk into a presentation and just wing it, thinking that Jesus will take care of it. We need to still do the proper training for whatever we are attempting. However, we also need to trust Jesus with the result.

After Jesus says that all things are possible for the person who believes, verse 24 says, "Immediately the father of the child cried out and said, 'I believe; help my unbelief!'"

We all need to be pushing boundaries of growth in our life. Pushing beyond our comfort zones. Pushing to believe beyond the line that marks where we've already seen accomplishments before. We must push ourselves into situations where we have not seen something done yet. And it is in exactly these places that we need to come humbly to God to ask for help with our unbelief. It is in these new areas where our faith can grow, and that is where we need to be.

We need to become comfortable with the uncomfortable. And when we are in the uncomfortable areas of our life, we need to put our faith and belief in God. When we do this, we grow in our faith. This is what makes our comfort zones get bigger. And this is what sets us up to have even greater experiences in the future.

ACTION STEPS

Spend five minutes writing down issues and situations you are worried or stressed about, including what you expect the outcome of these situations will be.

Now spend five minutes in prayer, asking God to help remove your fear and worry and to help with your unbelief. Also, pray for wisdom about how you can improve your chances of a positive outcome.

Write down any thoughts that come to mind on how you might improve the results. Now spend two minutes visualizing the upcoming situation, including an ending that reflects these positive results!

PRAYER

Lord, I want to be growing and pushing myself into new areas that will bump me up against my unbelief. Lord, I don't want to play it safe. I will work to visualize success in different areas I can tackle today that will help me with my unbelief. Amen.

9

HOW CAN YOU BE INTENTIONAL THIS SEASON?

Leadership Trait: Intentionality

Acts 18:11, "And he stayed a year and six months, teaching the word of God among them."

In chapter 18 of Acts, the Apostle Paul has arrived in Corinth, which was one of the political and commercial centers of Greece at that time. Like most cities today, Corinth had a mixture of good and high moral individuals as well as immoral and corrupt individuals. So as Paul was teaching the Good News of Jesus to the people of Corinth, there were people who were very receptive to what he was sharing and others who rejected his teaching, even to the point of insulting him.

Like you and me, Paul had his good days and his bad days as he interacted with others. Verse 9 tells us, "And the Lord said to Paul one night in a vision, 'Do not be afraid, but go on speaking and do not be silent.'" Paul was obedient to this command and stayed in Corinth for a year and six months, teaching the word of God, as verse 11 mentions.

However, it was not an easy eighteen months. There were days of frustration as some people rejected Paul's teaching. Even though Paul was being obedient and doing his job, he must have felt sometimes like he was swimming upstream. Plus, there was the frustration of waiting for God to reveal his next assignment.

I know one of the hardest things in my life is waiting for what will happen next. *When will I get the job? When will they call me back? Why is it taking so long?*

While I am waiting and wondering for the next development, I can start to get frustrated. Frustrated that I am not hearing anything about new steps to take. This then leads to feeling anxious about whether I am even in the right place or doing the right thing. What if I didn't hear God's signal and should have already moved on? All of these worries can sometimes move me into a place of slothfulness as I feel discouraged and wonder if my goal is even worth pursuing anymore. It's almost as if I'm thinking, *Fine, if it isn't going to happen, then I will just sit here.*

In chapter 1 of this book, I shared a story from about five years ago, when I was President of Sales for a company that went through a company sale process that was ultimately unsuccessful, as we did not find a buyer.

In preparation for the sale that didn't take place, we spent about six months gathering data and building presentations, as well as conducting the actual presentation and holding meetings with these potential buyers. But after all that hard work, we were back at the starting line.

I felt defeated. Lost. Discouraged.

Before that job, I had left a large company I'd worked at for ten years, where I'd eventually become a divisional Vice President, with many opportunities for future growth. However, I'd felt that I was called to this new job as part of my career advancement.

I started to have thoughts like, *Didn't you bring me here for this company sale? I thought the plan was to help build the company toward this transaction, then off to bigger and better things. What is going on, God?* Yet I didn't receive any answers to these random thoughts.

Months later, I was in Miami, Florida, making sales calls with our local sales team. From there, I was to drive to Tampa for a meeting with the leadership of the company and with the private equity group. As I was driving, I started to think again about this process of the failed company sale, as well as what it could mean for my future. What was I supposed to do now: stay or go?

I was to the point where I was crying out to God for answers. Literally praying out loud. Even yelling to God. "I thought this was going to be *my time*. My exit. My cash out. Why did you even bring me to this Florida company? Why did I leave a great company after ten years?"

You name it, I was probably saying it. Once again, not my finest moment. But once again, an honest one.

I started rattling off all kinds of thoughts: "Do I update my resume and get out of the company? Do I stick around for another company sale? Should I call other companies and look for a new job?"

Thoughts were running rampant through my head, both good and bad. Then out of nowhere, I heard an audible voice, or at least one that felt audible to me. Its message was very clear: *"Stay."*

"God is that you?" I asked. "'Stay'? Why? For how long? Are you sure? God, do you have any other words for me?"

I heard nothing else. Just the one word: "Stay."

Now I had more questions than answers. However, a sense of peace came over me. The stress and frustration even began to settle. Even though I didn't know entirely what the message meant in the long term, I felt that the obedient thing to do now would be to stay.

Over the coming months, our company's owners directed us to downsize, in order to keep our company profitable as they contemplated what to do next. During this time, I remember employees, and even my wife, asking if I was going to update my resume and look for a new job. I told them "no" and said that I felt called to stay.

Ironically, after receiving that direction, I no longer sat around discouraged. I now felt that God had a plan. I would be lying if I said I never wondered when I would receive another word. But I made a choice to keep moving forward until I heard differently.

During the time I spent operating under the word "stay," I had my good days and my bad days. I am sure this is how Paul felt in Acts 18:11 when he ended up staying in Corinth for a year and six months! Leading up to that moment, Paul had typically stayed in one place for a few days, or a few weeks at the most, to teach the Good News of Jesus before heading off to the next town. Paul had to be anxious at times during those eighteen months. I imagine he prayed something like, "God, if we are to spread this news, then I need to get to the next town. Haven't these people heard enough?"

However, he stayed and was obedient as he waited for God's next signal. During his time in Corinth, he continued to teach the gospel and impact many people who lived there. While Paul was waiting for the next signal, he was obedient and intentional.

HOW ARE YOU PREPARING THIS SEASON?

When we are in the waiting room of a doctor's office, we can choose to waste our time or be intentional with it. We can sit there and scroll mindlessly on our phone as we wait for our name to be called. Or we can work on some emails, pray about our day, listen to part of a podcast, or even set up our online grocery order.

The same thing is true when we are in a season of waiting for what is next. We can choose to waste time and just do the bare minimum at our job, or we can be very intentional and make the most of the moment.

During my time in the "waiting room," I doubled down on investing in my sales team. Not only did I work to help them meet their sales goals, I also taught them some of the life coaching skills I was learning, in order to help round them out as leaders. I also spent time investing in myself by exploring the idea of starting my own coaching and speaking business, by getting a few clients, and putting together content.

This continued for a few months. Then in August 2016 I was terminated from that job. However, I was not discouraged by this termination. God had already used that waiting time to prepare my mind and heart for the drastic change of leaving my corporate job, including my high salary and fancy title, and starting at ground zero of becoming a coach.

This transition was possible because God had softened my heart and helped break my reliance on both a corporate executive identity and a sense of financial security. I now realized instead that God was my provider. The truth is, I don't believe I ever would have started the coaching and speaking business if I hadn't been terminated and if I hadn't had the time in the "waiting room" to prepare my heart and mind.

Do you feel you are waiting for the next thing?

If we are not careful, we can miss out on beneficial waiting room time by wasting time instead of being intentional. However, when we believe that God uses all seasons to better us, we can experience the waiting room as a place where He is doing work in us and preparing us for what is on the other side of this season.

ACTION STEPS

Spend five minutes thinking of ways that you can be intentional during this season in the areas of both your personal and professional growth.

Now spend five minutes thinking of ways you can personally invest in those you lead and help them grow, both at work and at home. We need to make sure we are intentional in our leadership so that those we're leading are better for having had the opportunity to be led by us!

PRAYER

Lord, waiting rooms are frustrating, yet I know you use them for our good. I repent over the times I've gotten frustrated, and the times that frustration has turned into slothfulness. I will diligently spend my days investing in myself and those around me, so that we may grow closer to you and become better prepared to help you in your work. Amen.

10

HOW HAS GOD EQUIPPED YOU?

Leadership Trait: Strengths

1 Corinthians 1:31, "So that, as it is written, 'Let the one who boasts, boast in the Lord.'"

I must repent. There are times that I think my success is a direct result of my own efforts. Maybe you are the same way.

I won the sales trip because of my great sales skills.

I got the promotion because of my stellar leadership.

I received strong speaking endorsements because of my great speaking skills.

I landed the client because of my great business development.

I got the client to have a breakthrough because of my great coaching.

No. God did all of this! Yes, we each must steward well what was given to each of us. However, God did all of this. Not me.

God put the paying customers in front of me.

God surrounded me with a great team.

God gave me the insight and ideas to write the book.

God took my broken mess and restored it and then turned the whole thing into my message.

God gave me the desire to work with people.

God gave me the gift of confidence that makes it possible for me to speak in front of others.

None of the things I've accomplished were done on my own. Instead, God did it all and I often fail to give God the credit.

This posture of believing that I did it all, and that I must keep every piece of my life working, is exhausting. When I cling to this posture, it's like I'm running around in a panic, trying to keep a house of cards from falling. Yet when I am aware that God is the architect of my life, I am no longer concerned about keeping the house standing correctly. He is the one who built the house, and He will help keep it up. And He will be the architect of whatever will be built, or rebuilt, in its place.

Throughout the Bible there are numerous examples of God wanting to do life with us and of His desire that we not be left completely on our own. In Genesis 6, for instance, God provides Noah the dimensions to build the ark, and in Exodus 3 and 4,

God tells Moses the steps to take to help free the Israelites from the Egyptians. Psalm 55:22 tells us to "Cast your burden on the Lord, and he will sustain you; he will never permit the righteous to be moved."

Jesus continues this theme of wanting to help us by saying in Matthew 11:28–30, "Come to me, all who labor and are heavy laden, and I will give you rest. Take my yoke upon you, and learn from me, for I am gentle and lowly in heart, and you will find rest for your souls. For my yoke is easy, and my burden is light." These verses are just a few examples of God's desire to assist us.

As I work to build my business and lead my family, I find freedom in knowing that I don't have to do all the work. There are times, however, when I resist taking my stresses or struggles to God or sharing them with others, because I don't want to appear weak. I think, *If I am a successful executive coach for others, then I never should experience difficulties in my own business. If I am an author of a book called* Win at Home First, *then I should never experience struggles at home.*

You probably have similar feelings. Maybe you lead a team of 20 or 200 at work, yet you don't want to admit you are having trouble leading your two kids. Maybe you manage a 100 million dollar business, but you struggle with your own personal finances.

The reality is, we all struggle with elements of our business and home, and we need to have the courage to share our emotions and thoughts as we seek God's help in navigating these challenges. I love the numerous times in Psalms where David expresses his honest emotions, including discouragement (Psalm 13), fear (Psalm 23), and anger (Psalm 59). God wants us to share all our emotions with Him, just as David did. Even though we often view emotion as a weakness, it is a strength.

Realizing that leading my business and my family was not all on me was a breakthrough for me. Knowing that no one is expected to be good at all things is a form of grace. Yes, we have all been given certain gifts that we need to steward well. But we are also missing other gifts, and that is okay. As a matter of fact, it's more than okay. It is the way that we and the body of Christ are designed to be. If we all had every skill that we needed, then none of us would need God or others. Instead, in our weaknesses we must rely on other people, and on Him.

So, what are you good at? Is it strategy, numbers, communication, leadership, creativity, or something else? I personally love connecting with people and enjoy coaching and speaking to others. I have a strong work ethic and as an Enneagram #3, I can get stuff done! I am grateful the Lord gave me these gifts.

Now, what are you *not* good at? I personally am not handy, nor do I really have any desire to learn how to fix anything. The joke in our house is that after I try to hang up something, there will be ten holes left behind for that one piece of art! I have tried to learn other languages (Dutch for a work trip to the Netherlands and Spanish for a mission trip to Nicaragua), but learning a language was harder for me than for other people I know. And in the workplace, I can get bored easily, and I don't enjoy the small details of projects. I can be a great starter, but I'm not always strong at finishing.

It makes sense, then, that when I believe building my business and family is all on me, I get frustrated because I can't do those things. I see others who are good in areas of my deficiencies, and I can get bitter. Sometimes I can even start to think I don't have what it takes to succeed at their level.

You probably do the same as you compare yourself to others in your space. However, God has known from the beginning the great things you will accomplish, because He made you. I encourage you to leverage the skills you have. Do not get discouraged by anything you lack. Yes, we need to be curious and explore new skills and talents. And we all should want to be lifelong learners. However, we can't let our weaknesses stop us from accomplishing things using our current strengths.

God used Moses, a weak communicator, to lead the Israelites into the Promised Land. God used David, a small shepherd boy, to defeat a giant, and David eventually became king. There is a tribe, a team, a family who will follow the real you. Step into what you are currently good at. As you progress, then you can add skills and talents needed to become a better leader.

Often when I work with clients, I will have them think about the person they want to be in one year, three years, or five years. After we talk about what they wrote down, I then have them write down the skill sets they need to have in order to become that person.

For example, if you want to be an author, then you might start by writing blogs. You can then get feedback from others in that space regarding your work.

If you want to become a better leader, then have your boss and coworkers share with you one weak spot in your leadership skills or an area in which you need to grow. Once you've identified an area where you can grow—for example, empathy—then spend time watching videos or reading books on the topic.

You need not—and should not—build your business or your family on your own. By leaning on God and community instead, you can do life with others. Plus, you can reach out to others in your network to help you in a skill set that you do not have!

ACTION STEPS

Spend five minutes writing down all the strengths you currently have.

Next, spend two minutes taking notice and giving thanks to God for all that He has given you. This will help you to realize that we should only boast in the Lord, since He has given us all of our strengths!

Spend five minutes to think about who you want to be in one year, three years, or five years (or all three). Consider all the many areas of your life (work, home, marriage, parenting, friendships, etc.).

Now spend two minutes writing down the skills that future version of yourself will need.

Finally, think about one or two actions you can take now to grow in those skills.

BONUS: RISE AND GO MANIFESTO

The strengths that you listed can be the start of your "I am statements" in part 3 of your manifesto. For example, "I am an encourager." "I am a good starter to projects."

PRAYER

Lord, I repent of thinking my success is all on me. I want to stop doing that. You have gotten me this far using the talents you have given me. Thank you. I pray that I will stop chasing all the talents I don't have. I want to instead step into the talents I do have and use them to help expand your Kingdom. Lord, I also pray for wisdom to know the areas where I need to grow in order to become the leader I need to be and fulfill my future responsibilities. Amen.

11

WHERE DO YOU NEED TO BE BOLD?

Leadership Trait: Courage

Exodus 4:13, "But he said, 'Oh, my Lord, please send someone else.'"

Some days, I just want to hide. I want to stay in my office with the door shut. I just want to hide behind my computer and not talk to anyone.

Why is that?

On some days, it's simply because I am tired. However, there are other days when I feel that way because I am scared. Scared of exactly what, I don't always know. I suspect that I am both scared of success and scared of failure.

I am scared that what I am doing may cause me to become successful, and then I will have to work a lot more hours than I currently do. I fear that success may move me out of the comfortable life I currently know.

I'm also scared that I will fail. I don't want to fail. If I fail, I will have to admit that my coaching and speaking business was not a success and get another job. In my mind, failure means unpaid bills and the embarrassment of having to downsize everything in my life.

We can see fear play out in Moses's life too. In Exodus 3:10, Moses had just been told that he was God's chosen leader who would lead God's people from slavery in Egypt into the Promised Land. In the remaining part of chapter 3, God then gave Moses a plan of attack. In verse 16, he was instructed to go and gather the elders of Israel and tell them the plan to free them from Egypt. Then in verse 18, the elders and Moses were told to visit the king of Egypt and ask to be released.

Even with the benefit of this anointing from God and this detailed strategy, Moses was getting nervous again in verse 4:1. The crazy part is that God had just calmed down Moses's nerves in the previous chapter, at the burning bush, when Moses pushed back with the question, "Who am I?" (Exodus 3:11).

Once again, Moses's fears and doubts were starting to boil up. But why did his fears and doubts start to rise up again? I believe it was because Moses made a mistake that we all make, way too often: he started to think about what others would say.

Frequently, we spend more time thinking about what others will think of us than we do about our own ability—or, more importantly, God's ability. In Exodus 4:1, Moses said, "'But behold *they* will not believe me or listen to my voice'" (emphasis mine).

We get ourselves into trouble when we start to think about how others will respond. The reality is, there will always be naysayers, no matter how good our plan is. Focusing on doubts, however, can lead to us deciding not to move at all. Perhaps this is why God showed Moses three times the mighty power that He has, and that He would use through Moses.

In Exodus 4:2, God, said to Moses, "What is that in your hand?" Moses responded that he had "a staff." This exchange is a great reminder that we always need to return our focus to what is in our control, instead of wondering what others will think. We need to control the controllables. What other people think is not something we can control. Looking at what is in our hand, as Moses did, is part of controlling the controllables.

In the next series of verses, God demonstrated His power in three different ways. First, He had Moses throw the staff on the ground, at which point it turned into a serpent (v. 3). Second, He had Moses stick his hand inside his jacket. When he pulled his hand back out, it was "leprous like snow" (v. 6). Finally, God had Moses stick that same hand back into his jacket. When he pulled it out again, "it was restored like the rest of his flesh" (v. 7).

Yet even though Moses witnessed all those miracles, it was still not enough. He still had doubts in himself and God.

In Exodus 4:13, Moses said, "Oh, my Lord, please send someone else."

Oh, can I relate to this verse.

Sometimes, I spend too much time wondering what other people will think. *Will they say "yes" or "no" to me? Maybe I should turn down that speaking engagement. What if they think I am the worst speaker at the conference? Maybe I shouldn't host the event. What if people don't show up or don't have a great time?*

Then I start to doubt myself. *Will I sound smart? What if I am asked a question and don't know what to respond? Will I be exposed as someone who doesn't have all the answers?*

I also start to doubt God. *Will He abandon me? Is He in favor of this idea? What if He is thinking "Yes, but not now"?*

ONE STEP AT A TIME

My friend Kent Wellington, an attorney in Cincinnati, has helped launch two non-profits: Saturday Hoops and the Karen Wellington Foundation for LIVING with Breast Cancer. Saturday Hoops brings basketball and a program of encouragement to inner city neighborhoods. The Karen Wellington Foundation for LIVING with Breast Cancer, named after his wife who passed away from cancer, helps women who are battling cancer by putting some fun in their life. Their organization mission states, "Our mission is simple. We send women and families LIVING with breast cancer on special vacations, relaxing spa days, concerts, and other FUN-ONLY activities." Both programs are amazing and have been going strong for more than fifteen years.

Scan QR code to listen to the podcast

In an interview on my "Win at Home First" podcast, Kent stated that he found one of the non-profit organizations, and the other one found him. The first was Saturday Hoops that he helped launch with two other guys. Kent had been a college athlete, so playing basketball on Saturdays and including his two kids in the activities seemed like an easy lift in his mind. His thoughts early on were that he could just show up, invest in these kids to help them be "cheerful givers, hard workers and overcomers," play some basketball, and see where things went from there. Obviously, there is much more to the story. But the point is, he viewed this outreach with somewhat rose-colored glasses from the beginning.

The Karen Wellington Foundation for LIVING with Breast Cancer was a different story. Kent feels the foundation found him, since he had no intention of ever starting a foundation for cancer. After his wife passed away, he received a phone call asking where to send the flowers for the funeral. As he sat there, he recalled a conversation that he had with his wife years prior when she said one day after chemo treatment, "after we beat cancer, wouldn't it be cool if we could go on a vacation each year and send someone else living with cancer on a vacation too?" Unfortunately, they never got to send others on vacations during the ten years they lived with cancer. So during that phone call, he decided that instead of flowers, people could send money and they would use that money to send a family fighting cancer on a vacation. That led to one family, then two families, all while bringing on more questions. How would the outreach organize vacations for all those families? Where would the donations needed to fund the vacations come from? How would they get access to the vacation properties the families would stay at? Plus, since Kent was an attorney, all kinds of legal questions and concerns were starting to swirl in his head.

But as he says, he found the Saturday Hoops non-profit, and the Karen Wellington Foundation for LIVING with Breast Cancer non-profit found him. He needed to make it work, but could he trust that God would be with him? This was a burning bush moment for Kent. In the early days, as he was still wondering whether to launch this foundation, Kent's response could have been, "Please send someone else."

However, he kept moving forward. He could not allow himself to get too overwhelmed with what *could* happen because he had a full-time job as an attorney, was now a single parent to two kids, and now had two non-profits to run. Yet he knew God had called him to build both non-profits, so he just had the time and energy to focus on one step at a time.

With the Karen Wellington Foundation for LIVING with Breast Cancer, that meant getting the first family on a vacation, then the second, and then the third. Today, they have ten chapters throughout the United States plus several ambassador cities, and they have given almost 2,000 gifts of fun to families living with cancer!

This is an incredible story. But not all ideas we pursue turn out to be this successful. Some ideas that God gives us are just building blocks that He intends us to use for something down the road. By being obedient and pursuing these ideas, we build character and perseverance. We also learn from our mistakes. In the business world, this is often referred to as "failing forward."

If we are to receive opportunities that will lead to success or to failing forward, we need to go into all our meetings, conversations, and quiet times with open hands, so that we are prepared to receive anything that God has for us. If we go in with closed fists instead, we will miss out on what God has in store for us.

Finally, once we receive the idea, then we need to pursue it with the right mindset. We need to act with peace in our hearts and trust that God, who has chosen us for the task, will be with us each step of the way.

ACTION STEPS

Spend ten minutes reviewing your current to-do list, as well as any to-do lists you have made so far while working through the exercises of this book. Consider these questions:

- On which items are you dragging your feet?
- Are there items that you have not even put on the list because of fear?

Now spend five minutes thinking of action steps you can take today to move some of these ideas forward. Write them down and, if you feel prompted to do so, schedule some of these steps in your calendar.

PRAYER

Lord, I can point to a few times when it was hard for me to say "yes" to you, yet things turned out awesome in the end. Thank you for those times! There are also times when I said "no" because I chickened out. I got in my own head. I cared too much about what others would think. Lord, please forgive me for the times when I was not obedient. I pray that I will be obedient to your call today. Amen.

12

HOW DO YOU HANDLE "NO"?

Leadership Trait: Rejection

Luke 10:2, "And he said to them, 'The harvest is plentiful, but the laborers are few. Therefore pray earnestly to the Lord of the harvest to send out laborers into his harvest.'"

There was a time when, if a prospect said "no" to my product or services, I would be devastated. Sometimes I took the answer personally, as if the decision was about me. Even if I didn't take the decision personally, I felt scared that I would not make my numbers for that month.

Maybe you can relate. Picture this. You worked hard to get a prospect to meet with you, and now it's your opportunity to give them your sales pitch. The day of the meeting has finally arrived. You meet the prospect in person or start up the Zoom call. You exchange the nice pleasantries and then dive into your sales script. The prospect shares their challenges and explains how long they have been dealing with them. You ask what other methods they have tried to overcome their challenge.

Finally, it is your turn to speak. You do a great job of explaining how your product or service will solve their problems and help them achieve their desired results. Then comes the moment when you ask if they are ready to buy. The prospect pauses and then says, "no." Or they say "no" in a less direct way: "Let me think about it."

What? Why? You think to yourself, *My product will solve their problem. My service is the best one out there.* You may be right. However, they said "no," and you feel defeated. After getting that response, it can be hard to get back out there and try again.

About ten years ago, the story in Luke 10 of Jesus sending out the disciples led me to a breakthrough in my sales mindset, and I pray that it helps you as well. Don't get me wrong—I still can feel defeated from time to time when a prospect says "no," because I am a competitor and want to win. Plus, I love to serve and help others. However, this teaching has allowed me to change my relationship with rejection and be able to shake off the "no" and get back to reaching out to prospects sooner than I used to.

In this passage in Luke, Jesus is sending out the seventy-two disciples in groups of two, to share the Good News with everyone in the community. Jesus sent out disciples to see if people were interested in hearing the gospel. He was looking to see who was open to hearing the greatest truth ever told to mankind. Of course, he wasn't pitching a product, he was looking to see who was open to hearing—which is what we're doing too, albeit in a different way.

The seventy-two disciples were instructed to knock on doors to see if the people at home would receive them. If the people invited the disciples into their house, then the disciples were to proceed: they were to go into the house and share the Good News with the people who were there. However, if the people in the home did not invite them in, then they were to shake the dust off their feet and move on to the next house. Yes, even the disciples who were spreading the Good News of Jesus were rejected!

What I find interesting is that Jesus knew there would be rejection. Yet He didn't tell the disciples to stay and try to convince whoever was home, or to beg them to listen. Instead, Jesus told the disciples to move on to the next house.

There was a time in my sales career when I would work extremely hard to try and convince engineers that they needed to add the product my company made to their job specifications. Or I would work hard to convince a contractor that my company's product needed to be purchased for their construction projects. Yet in Luke 10:2, when Jesus sent His disciples off, He said, "The harvest is plentiful, but the laborers are few."

The same is true of your businesses. People will say "no" to your business, no matter how much due diligence you have done or how strong your messaging is, even if you have identified them as your ideal client.

I am a big fan of sales guru Jeffrey Gitomer, and years ago I got to hear him speak. At his sales seminar, he said that in his industry, he needed to get seven "no's" before getting one "yes." So whenever he got a "no," he would say to himself, "Woo-hoo! I am now one 'no' closer to my 'yes'!"

If we are not getting enough "yes's" to meet our sales projections and keep ourselves financially stable, then we need to review and tweak our process or script, or maybe even the product or service all together, to make sure it is ready for the market. This verse does not give us permission to be sloppy.

However, Jeffrey's story serves as a good reminder to me, and to you. Not everyone will say "yes" to you. The truth is, not everyone is saying "yes" to your competitor either. Heck, not even Jesus got a "yes" from everyone! So when we receive a "no," we need to shake the dust off our feet and move on to the next prospect. Our mindset needs to be that there is an abundance of customers out there and be able to say, "On to the next one."

DON'T TAKE IT PERSONALLY

As I mentioned, there were times earlier in my sales career when I would tie the success or failure of my sales efforts to my identity. I would take my results personally, thinking that if I did well, then I was *the man*. If I was doing badly, I would fear that I deserved to get canned. If I am being honest, a focus on my identity has been my kryptonite throughout most of my life.

In high school, I wondered what the popular group thought.

In college, my issue was wondering what the fraternity guys thought.

In corporate America, it was wondering what the CEO thought of me.

Then I wondered what the private equity group thought of me.

Today, I wonder what clients will think of my content.

At every stage of life, there are moments where we look to affirmations and praise that are coming from humans and not from God. The above is just a short list of places I have turned to with my questions about my identity and worth. The actual list is much longer—embarrassingly so. However, turning to these places isn't productive, and relying on them for feedback on our identity will only take us on a volatile emotional ride.

I like how Jeff Bezos, founder and former CEO of Amazon, says it: "When the stock is up 30 percent in a month, don't feel 30 percent smarter, because when the stock is down 30 percent in a month, it's not going to feel so good to feel 30 percent dumber—and that's what happens."[11] The stock of Amazon will always fluctuate, as all stocks do. Jeff is warning his employees they cannot take the success or failure of the stock personally. If they do so, they will only be putting themselves on an emotional roller coaster.

I see this often in my coaching and speaking business as I engage with my clients. Many of us can take the feedback of customers, employees, or even family members personally and begin to tie that feedback to our identity. The identity we should all have is that we are sons or daughters of God. Yet many of us can take our identity from temporary roles instead, such as the success or failure we experience in various areas of our lives.

Stuart Tattum, a partner with an IT firm that specializes in helping retail companies, experienced this shock to his identity and mindset a few years ago. Even though Stuart knew that his real identity was that he was a beloved son of God, he found himself linking some of his identity to how his customers treated him.

Around that time, Stuart sold a project to a new customer and discovered within a few months that the amount of work required to complete the project was significantly more than the original estimate. The customer was not willing to pay for all of the additional work. In addition to not wanting to pay for all the work required, the customer was very challenging to work with and frequently expressed dissatisfaction with the work of Stuart and his team.

These events took a toll on Stuart's identity. Stuart had always received great feedback from customers before. But this time, the customer was not pleased with how the project had been going. It cost a significant amount of time, energy, and money for Stuart to complete the project for the customer.

Stuart was crushed. He thought he had lost his edge and the value he brought to customers. This conclusion sent Stuart into a mindset tailspin. He even reduced doing business development and

---

11   Jeff Bezos, quoted by Brad Stone, *The Everything Store* (New York: Little, Brown & Co., 2014).

was reluctant to reach out to new prospects and existing customers about new projects.

As you can imagine, reducing business development will catch up to you eventually! Stuart was a client of mine, and one of his concerns was the future of his business. As we discussed his business, we talked about the lack of a pipeline, or future work that he had coming up. It was during these conversations that I learned that he had reduced doing business development when this existing customer had not paid for all of the additional work.

Stuart and I then revisited what had happened with this customer and worked to untangle what was true from what was untrue. I had him list all the lies that he was telling himself about this situation, using journaling assignments. During our coaching calls, we then discussed each of those lies and explored what the actual truth was.

For example, one lie Stuart had come to believe was that he was no longer able to bring value to his customers. In his mind, this meant that he should not engage with any new customers. We discussed the truth that this one customer had in fact decided not to pay for all of the services to complete the project. Yet he had numerous customers who were pleased with his work and still enjoyed working with him and were willing to pay for the work.

Like many of us do from time to time, Stuart had created the lie by exaggerating the problem in his head, and then he'd started to believe it!

Through this process, we worked together to elevate Stuart's mindset and got him doing business development again, even leading to his best year of his career in 2021.

All of us will hear "no" at some time or another: whether we are trying to sell a customer something for the first time or the millionth time. We cannot tie this "no" to our identity. We cannot let it defeat us. Instead, we need to be expectant, knowing both good and bad things will happen. We need to trust that the harvest is plentiful and filled with numerous potential customers—and believe there is a "yes" waiting for us right around the corner!

ACTION STEPS

Spend five minutes thinking about any recent rejections that you have experienced.

Which prospects said "no" to your offer? What pushback have you recently experienced, personally or professionally? Have you received any critique or criticism? What lies are you believing based on these "no's"?

Now consider how you can improve your performance or product using the feedback these "no" responders gave you. It's important to make sure you are not tying your identity to any of their feedback or critique, but rather finding ways to learn from it.

BONUS: RISE AND GO MANIFESTO

The truths that you wrote down above can go into your Rise and Go Manifesto under part 3— "I Am Statements." For example, Stuart could write, "I provide great service to my customers" in his section. What truths can you add to your manifesto?

PRAYER

Lord, thank you for this story of Jesus sending out the seventy-two disciples. This story reminds me that people say "no" even to you. I am glad I said "yes" to you, and I want to continue to live a life of saying "yes" to you daily. I find hope in this verse, which reminds me that people will say both "yes" and "no" to my asks. While I need to continue to work to get the "yes," I need not be defeated by the "no's." Thank you for this reminder, for my job, and for your provision. Amen.

13

WHO IS YOUR PROVIDER?

Leadership Trait: Provision

Luke 19:16, "The first came before him, saying, 'Lord, your mina has made ten minas more.'"

In 2 Corinthians 12:7, Paul said he "was given a thorn in my flesh" (NIV), which remained all his life. Many experts have speculated about whether this was a metaphoric reference to some physical issue, like bad eyesight; a mental thorn, such as doubt; or a spiritual thorn, such as a temptation to a particular sin. No matter what it was, the thorn was such a constant annoyance to Paul that he said in 2 Corinthians 12:8, "Three times I pleaded with the Lord about this, that it should leave me."

Like Paul, we all have thorns in our life. The distractions they cause can sometimes keep us from aligning our hearts and minds with God's.

One of the thorns of my flesh is my relationship with money. There have been moments throughout my life where I've thought that all the financial burden lay on me and that God was not at work. Sometimes I even felt that He had abandoned me.

One of these times was when my mom died of cancer when I was in high school. During the last few years of her illness, my dad experienced some job changes and even job loss, causing our family's finances to be very tight. So when it was time for me to go to college, I had to take out college loans and get a part-time job for a stint. It was during that time that the devil started to whisper in my ear the lie that "It is all on me."

Another example is that just before the recession of 2008, my wife and I bought seven real estate properties. The subsequent Great Recession, as it has been called, caused a surplus in homes, drove the rental prices down, drove vacancies up. As a result, we were not able to experience a positive month-to-month cash flow from our rentals. We then experienced such issues as renter turn-over, storm damage, and wear and tear on the properties, and so racked up significant credit card debt. All the while, the devil kept telling me that improving our situation was all on me.

A few years later, I learned some astonishing truths. Though I didn't see it at the time, God had been at work in both of those examples. He had not abandoned me all!

As for my family's financial challenges when I was in high school, I eventually learned that the church we attended at that time paid my family's mortgage for a year while my mom was sick! God had indeed been at work!

As for our real estate debacle, in time my wife and I saw God at work there as well. It so happened that a few years after the market started to unravel, we were running out of money. We continued to receive endless calls from creditors, and we felt we were running out of time and options. We decided to meet with a bankruptcy attorney to get out of this mess.

Then, while we were sitting in the bankruptcy attorney's office,

I heard a prompting from God. In my mind I heard Him saying: *I will get you out of this. There is another way.*

What? I wondered. Nothing had been working the last few years! What was different now? What was the other way?

Though my wife and I didn't how God would get us out of this mess, we had faith God was at work. We decided to not file for bankruptcy. Shortly afterward, through some incredible surprises—such as an unexpected promotion and bonus, plus financial support from loved ones—we were able to climb out of our financial woes. Once again, God was at work!

TWO SIMILAR PARABLES WITH ONE KEY DIFFERENCE

Such yo-yo-like ups and downs with money have been a constant tension in my life. You may experience that tension as well. But in April 2020, my good friend Ray shared a YouTube teaching on the Parable of the Ten Minas that changed my perspective on money, and possibly my whole life! The video was titled "Day 3—Nehemiah Prayer/Fast" by Zebulun Strategies.[12] In the video, J. R. Fitch and Marco Leardini explain the difference between the Parable of the Talents (Matthew 25:14–30) and the Parable of the Ten Minas (Luke 19:11–27).

As I shared in chapter 2, my revenue had dropped by 35 percent in April 2020, and I did not see how I was going to get out of the situation. Once again, the devil was back, whispering *It's all on you* constantly in my head. I needed help and a change in my money perspective. This video was just the message I needed, and it came at just the right time.

Both the Parable of the Talents and Parable of Ten Minas tell about masters who gave their servants a certain amount of money. The talent and the mina were forms of currency that were used in the Middle East and Greece thousands of years ago. Per the ESV

12 Zebulun Strategies, "Day 3—Nehemiah Prayer/Fast," April 7, 2020, https://www.youtube.com/watch?v=Ktf22KVfeSc.

Bible translation, a talent was a monetary unit worth about twenty years of wages for a laborer, whereas the mina was about three months of wages for a laborer.

In the Parable of the Talents, the master gave one servant five talents, another servant received two talents, and a third servant received one talent. In the Parable of the Ten Minas, the master gave ten of his servants, ten minas.

In both parables, when the master returned, some servants reported that they had earned a positive return on the money, while others reported that they buried their money out of fear. However, there is a subtle difference in word choice between the two parables. This difference is what made a major impact on me.

In the Parable of the Talents, the servants who reported a profit said, "Look what *I* have done." Whereas in the Parable of Ten Minas, the servants said, "Look what *your* mina has done." (Emphasis in both cases is mine.)

I versus *Your*. One word difference, but enormous mindset difference. The first quote is all about selfishness. The second one is about stewardship. The first is all about getting. The second, about receiving.

A mindset that tells us something is all on us leads to a scarcity mindset that says, "I have to do all the work." When times are good, this can cause us to get prideful, and when times are bad, we become very discouraged and lose hope.

One the other hand, when we realize the issue is one of stewardship, then we remember that God is in control. This mindset leads to more freedom and to the hope that God will provide again, just as He has in the past.

This recognition of "I" versus "Your" was the start of my perspective change. However, the turning point for me was seeing how the master rewarded the servants differently in the two parables.

In the Parable of the Talents, the master just gave his servants additional money. However, in the Parable of Ten Minas, instead of giving the first two servants more money, he gave them more power and responsibility! The servant who made five minas out of one mina was given authority over five cities. The servant who made ten minas out of one mina was given authority over ten cities. Cities instead of money!

When God sees we are stewarding the resources we have been given, treating them as His and not ours, He provides greater rewards. I believe, though, that when we become prideful and believe our success is all about us, He limits what He gives.

The question isn't just one of pride, though. It's also one of connection. The Lord wants to grow in relationship with us, and when we are hustling for our own money, then we are not in relationship with God. When we assume the posture that we are stewarding his resources, however, then our efforts become more about partnership.

I got to see this firsthand when my first book was published in Germany. I had tried and tried to sell books, and I had indeed been blessed with some success. But having a book published in Germany was absolutely a God thing, and the story of random connections that led to that development proves it.

The story begins in California in October 2019, when I met a businesswoman named Kimberly while at a BAM (Business as Mission) conference. Kimberly and I had a great conversation, and I ended up giving her a copy of my book, *Win at Home First*.

To my surprise, when we ran into each other two days later at the conference, she had already read my book and had highlighted parts of it! I couldn't believe she'd read my book in two days, while attending a conference. But there was still another surprise in store for me: Kimberly wanted to introduce me to Benjamin, a businessman from Germany, who was also at the conference.

After she introduced us, Benjamin and I had a nice conversation. To be honest, I didn't see the connection going anywhere beyond that moment. I live in the United States, he lives in Germany. You get the point. However, when he got back to Germany, Benjamin happened to have a meeting with Gloria, who shared with him that she felt God had put it on her heart to publish an American Christian book in German!

Benjamin shared my book and message with Gloria and got us connected. After a few conversations between Gloria and me, and after a lot of work done by Gloria's publishing company, *Win at Home First* was published in the German language in 2021!

Since this was such a crazy story of connections that only God could orchestrate, I began telling myself of an important truth by using the following phrase: *I control the input and God controls the impact.*

I can only control what I can control. It's up to me to write the content, publish the book, and work hard to make connections, but ultimately, the impact of that book is up to God. God will choose how He wants to use all our efforts in the world. Yes, we must put in the work of stewarding His resources well. But we also must know that how God chooses to use the resources is up to Him.

To this day, my mindset about money is not perfect. However, I do a much better job now of not defining myself by the impact of the business. Instead, my responsibility financially is to have that mindset of *Your mina, not mine.*

Whatever financial work you're doing—whether that's managing your family finances or preparing the company's Profit and Loss statement—put yourself in the mindset of knowing that the mina is God's, and you are just stewarding it.

ACTION STEPS

Spend five minutes thinking and journaling about your mindset on money. Is the money you manage yours or God's? Do you have a scarcity mindset or abundance mindset? Do you see yourself or God as the provider?

Spend ten minutes writing down some of the wild stories of happenings in your business that only God could have orchestrated.

BONUS: RISE AND GO MANIFESTO

The stories you wrote down about the places where God showed up and showed off in your life can go into the part 6, "God Has the Nightshift" section of your manifesto. These are great stories to read from time to time, to be reminded of how God is working behind the scenes in your life.

PRAYER

Lord, thank you for great teachings like the Parable of Ten Minas that opened my eyes to your message about stewardship. I pray that I will treat the resources you give me as yours and not mine. Today I am stewarding your mina and not just hustling for my own. Amen.

PART 3

GO

Move Forward with Confidence

14

WHAT ARE YOU PRAYING FOR?

Leadership Trait: Goals

1 Chronicles 4:10, "Jabez called upon the God of Israel, saying, 'Oh that you would bless me and enlarge my border, and that your hand might be with me, and that you would keep me from harm so that it might not bring me pain!' And God granted what he asked."

The above verse from 1 Chronicles is often referred to as the Prayer of Jabez. Some people view this prayer as an example of prosperity gospel and say that we should not pray for the success of our businesses and lives. Other great spiritual leaders, like best-selling author and pastor Mark Batterson, have a different perspective. In his best-selling book, *The Circle Maker: Praying Circles Around Your Biggest Dreams and Greatest Fears*, Batterson says, "Bold prayers honor God, and God honors bold prayers."[13] I think the truth about whether the Prayer of Jabez is greedy or not lies in the heart of the person praying it.

If you are praying in pursuit of glory for your name, your treasures, and your wealth, then, yes: the prayer will be a greedy one. However, if the motivation behind your prayer is to bring God glory and impact the lives of others, then that prayer is a Kingdom-worthy prayer. We want our prayers to be such that God will see us as He saw David, whom Samuel called "a man after his [God's] own heart" (1 Samuel 13:14).

Unfortunately, I have experienced both versions of this prayer. I know that there are days when my prayer is rooted in greed—when I am asking God to do things like grow *my* business, help sell more of *my* books, and get *me* more clients. These are prayers rooted in selfishness and greed.

Yet there are other days when I am much more aligned with God, when my greatest desire is for the Lord to use me to impact other leaders and to help them grow closer to Him. In those moments, I pray that my book can help others to reorganize their priorities and live their lives more fully, even if they never hire me. I pray to find leaders who need a breakthrough in their lives, and I pray for the wisdom to help them.

This also applies to leading my family at home. I pray for discernment about what and when to share with my kids about God and Scripture so that they will be receptive and not roll their eyes at me! I want to make sure what I share with my kids is timely and helpful, and not an example of me forcing the Bible on them while trying to check the box of being a good and godly parent.

Here's one example of how God helped me learn to turn my heart toward His plan. Two years ago a woman at my church spoke a prophetic word over me. She saw "a beautiful, wide-open field that only God could create."

---

13 Mark Batterson, *The Circle Maker: Praying Circles Around Your Biggest Dreams and Greatest Fears* (Grand Rapids: Zondervan, 2011), 15.

I believe she was speaking words from God, but I couldn't figure out what it meant.

"*A beautiful, wide-open field* . . ." What was this? Was I going to be a farmer? Was I going to go live somewhere out in the country? Anyone who knows me understands that would be a miracle in itself! Maybe, I thought, this was a reference to business, and the open field referenced market opportunity. But that didn't seem probable, since coaching and speaking is a very saturated market, so it was far from a wide-open field.

The second part, "*that only God can create,*" also brought confusion. What did that mean? Was I not supposed to invest financially in my business, such as by placing social media ads? Maybe I was not supposed to hire any consultants or partners to help me grow the business. But that didn't seem feasible or wise, as I knew that God wants us to help one another grow.

Initially, I could not make sense of the prophetic words at all. As I spent some time thinking and praying about it, however, the word *field*, started to jump out to me. One day it hit me to turn the word into an acronym, FIELD, and explore the values that each letter might represent. I did so, and for the last two years I have been praying the resulting prayer a couple times a week. I don't know if God intended for me to get my own customized Prayer of Jabez from that prophetic moment. I occasionally revisit the "beautiful, wide-open field that only God can create" vision with hopes of learning more, though so far, I haven't received any more clarity. However, I *have* enjoyed the prayer that came out of the field image, as well as the focus it brings me.

Following is the outline of the prayer I have been using. Feel free to adopt it for yourself or modify as you see fit.

F. *Favor*—I pray for God's favor on my family members and on our interactions with others. I pray that my business will grow and that I will have opportunities to impact others. I pray that my clients, their families, and their businesses will prosper.

I. *Intimacy with God*—I pray that I will grow closer to God daily through Scripture reading, prayer, and the adoption of the mindset of *God's glory and not mine.* I pray for the pursuit of God's plan and not mine. I pray to remember *God's mina and not mine.* I pray to grow closer to God so that my heart will align with His.

E. *Expand*—I pray for the expansion of my business, territory, and impact; for new markets and cities to go into; for new companies and clients to reach. I pray to reach readers and listeners in new countries with my books and podcast. I pray that God will expand my family's reach through personal connections, academics and sports.

L. *Love my enemy*—I pray for my competitors. I pray for prospects who say "no." I pray for people who may frustrate or irritate me. (In Matthew 5:44 Jesus says, "Love your enemies and pray for those that persecute you." If I am not careful, my competitive side can cause me to think wrongly of my competition and of those who don't agree with me, so I have decided to take a proactive approach to pray for them. This simple yet hard act has helped me right my posture regarding my competition!)

D. *Deliver me from evil*—I pray that God will deliver me from greed, lust for more, envy, jealousy, and lack of self-control. I keep a list of the sins that I battle with most and call them out each day.

The FIELD prayer is not a prayer that every person must pray. However, I have experienced breakthroughs and freedom as a result of this prayer helping to align my heart to God's. This prayer has assisted me in keeping my mindset consistent with the pursuit of God's glory. And it has helped me to repent and walk away from sins that are getting in the way of my relationship with God.

I do believe God answers our prayers when they are aligned with Him and meet His timing, whether that prayer is the Prayer of Jabez or a homemade one like my FIELD prayer. I like how the book of James talks about this in the New Living Translation. James writes a letter addressed to the members of the twelve tribes who had either fled or had been exiled from Jerusalem. In it, he talks to them about their wants, needs, and prayers:

"You want what you don't have, so you scheme and kill to get it. You are jealous of what others have, but you can't get it, so you fight and wage war to take it away from them. Yet you don't have what you want because you don't ask God for it. And even when you ask, you don't get it because your motives are all wrong—you want only what will give you pleasure" (James 4: 2–3 NLT).

Wow!

I know those of us reading this are not killing anybody or waging war, though our greed and envy can still bring out the worst in us in our actions and motives. Yet the last sentence clearly speaks to all of us. Our prayers are often about our own pleasure. They are about "me" and not others.

Yes, we can pray for aspects of our life to grow. But God can tell whether our prayers are sparked by selfish motives or a desire to bless others along the way. We need to start praying boldly instead for things in our lives that will bring glory to God and will help us to participate in expanding the Kingdom.

ACTION STEPS

Spend five minutes thinking about your prayer life and write down answers to these questions, along with any other thoughts that come to mind.

- What do you most often pray for?
- What are some prayers you can pray that are bold yet also honor God?

Spend five minutes praying for what you want, remembering that bold prayers honor God!

PRAYER

Lord, I pray for you to do great things in my business and in my life. However, I pray even more that my heart will align with yours so that I may build my business and life in ways that bring you honor and glory. I don't want to fall victim to the ways of this world. I want to instead build a business and life that reflects your ways. Amen.

15

WHAT ARE YOU THINKING ABOUT?

Leadership Trait: Mindset

Philippians 4:8, "Finally, brothers, whatever is true, whatever is honorable, whatever is just, whatever is pure, whatever is lovely, whatever is commendable, if there is any excellence, if there is anything worthy of praise, think about these things."

Here is a statement I strongly believe that some people may have trouble accepting: We all have the power to control our thoughts. I'm not saying that I believe we *create* all our thoughts. I am saying, though, that we can control them. Our minds are battlefields, and Satan is always trying to gain ground by firing off arrows of self-doubt, negative talk, and self-limiting beliefs that will knock us off our feet. Think about it. When are we the biggest threat to Satan? When we believe in ourselves! Because that is when we're best positioned to expand God's Kingdom.

When we are confident, we are more likely to respond to the Holy Spirit's nudge to pray for someone, to go out of our way to talk to our neighbor, to leave a larger tip for the server at dinner, or to be vulnerable by putting our work out into the public. On the other hand, when we are discouraged, we often ignore the Holy Spirit's promptings—if we even notice the promptings at all! When we are feeling down, we don't want to talk to anyone about anything of significance. And so we do our best to keep conversations at surface level, even though we recognize that there is an opportunity to go deeper.

A person's thought life is a great indicator of the success he or she will experience in life. For thousands of years, historical philosophers and thinkers, as well as today's thought leaders, have made important observations regarding the power of our thoughts.

The Bible has many verses that address a person's thinking. One popular one is Proverbs 21:2: "Every way of a man is right in his own eyes, but the Lord weighs the heart." (ESV)

The famous Stoic and Roman Emperor Marcus Aurelius (160–180 AD) wrote: "A man's life is what his thoughts make of it."

The famous nineteenth-century philosopher and poet Ralph Waldo Emerson wrote: "A man is what he thinks about all day long."

A popular voice from the 1950s, author Earl Nightingale said: "We become what we think about."

More recently, John Maxwell, an internationally recognized leadership expert, speaker, and author who has sold over 19 million books, said, "You go where your thoughts go."

I find all these quotes helpful. But even more helpful to me over these last two years, in terms of applying these ideas in my own life, is a concept that was introduced to me by Travis Peters, who served as a mentor and coach to me for a few months in 2020, when I was a student in a coaching program to help grow my business. I don't know who originated the concept, but the idea goes something like this: "Our thoughts lead to our feelings, which lead to our actions, which lead to our results." Travis shared this as a series of two separate cycles.

CYCLE OF AWESOME

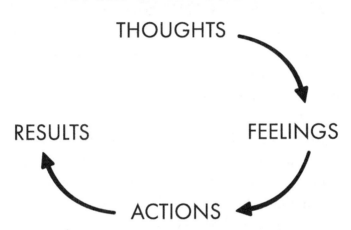

THOUGHTS

RESULTS   FEELINGS

ACTIONS

The first one is called the "Cycle of Awesome." When we start the day with positive thoughts, then we feel upbeat and are in good spirits. This upbeat feeling gives us a feeling of confidence in who we are and excitement to go after our day, which then leads us to take positive actions. On the business side, those actions could include great sales calls. In our personal lives, this might look like encouraging encounters with our spouse or kids.

When you are having great encounters with clients and/or family members, then the results of those encounters will more than likely be positive. If we are to create this kind of flow, it is critical that we start our day with positive thoughts. Doing this is likely to yield positive results.

Scan QR code to listen to the podcast

Jim Samocki, President of Doran Manufacturing, shared on my podcast that he starts every day by getting out of bed and saying, "Make it a great day." Jim knows that our thoughts drive our actions. So instead of repeating the all-too-common phrase, "Have a great day," he starts the day by taking ownership of his thoughts and saying, "Make it a great day!"

If we start off with negative thoughts, then we know we will have negative results. If we wake up grumpy or with a victim mentality, we intuitively know that day is not going to end very well. Obviously, we all wake up that way from time to time. There is no shame in that. The purpose of this book is simply to give you tools you can use to recalibrate your mind so that you can change your perspective and start to think better thoughts!

One thing that trips us up, however, is that we sometimes start our day off by looking for results even before we take time to formulate any positive thoughts! This is called the "Cycle of Awful."

CYCLE OF AWFUL

RESULTS

ACTIONS   THOUGHTS

FEELINGS

For example, instead of starting my day with positive thoughts, I might grab my phone and immediately look at my email and social media. If I see anything less than a prospect saying, "Yes, I want to start" or a post of mine that has gone viral overnight, I can be disappointed. I will then start my day off feeling defeated and discouraged. I'll imagine that my business is not taking off and that what is ahead is just another hard day of swimming upstream.

It doesn't have to be a dive into social media or email. Some people look at their company's sales results from the day before. Some look at their personal finances from the day before. Others look to the news first thing when they grab their phone.

When we start looking to the world's results—whether related to money, news, or social media—then we allow those things to shape our thoughts. This is usually not helpful. Very rarely do we ever turn to these outlets and then get excited and feel fired up to start our day!

I know that the way I start my day—whether thinking positive thoughts or looking for results—will affect how I respond to my circumstances. This includes how I respond when a prospect tells me "no."

If I start my day with bad thoughts that are based on a lack of results, I can let that "no" fester. The result is that I will start to build up additional bad thoughts about my business. These might be as drastic and ridiculous as, "I am never going to get another client." More often, the negative thought is smaller, along the lines of, "I may not get another client this week," or "This month is going to be an awful revenue month."

Eventually, these negative thoughts turn into bad feelings. We get discouraged, our self-confidence shrinks, and we may even become depressed. These bad feelings lead to weak actions because we are not motivated. We lose focus at work, become easily distracted, and eventually stop doing any significant work because we are discouraged.

These negative feelings will have a ripple effect in other areas of my life. I will start to hit the snooze button and skip gym workouts. I will start to make poor food choices, and thus get more sluggish. I will be less joyful to be around as a spouse, parent, and friend.

These bad actions further lead to bad results. When I have a meeting with a prospect during one of these sluggish times, I am not as confident and upbeat. At this point, the Law of the Mirror comes into effect: this is the concept that other people can feel our energy and even mirror it. Others will feel my lack of confidence, and so they too will lack confidence in me and my programs. This will lead more of them to say "no" to my coaching. Ironically, these negative thoughts end up becoming a self-fulfilling prophecy! What I imagine will be a bad month does in fact turn out to be a bad month.

CONTROLLING OUR THOUGHTS

So how do we control our thoughts and turn this around? Paul's words showed me two ways we can control our thoughts. First, he talks about focusing on "whatever is true, whatever is honorable, whatever is just, whatever is pure, whatever is lovely, whatever is commendable" (Philippines 4:8).

One action I have found to be helpful over the years is writing down the negative thoughts I hear in my head and then looking to Scripture to see what God's truth on the matter is. One such negative thought is, *I will never get another prospect and therefore my business will tank.* The truth is that my business will not tank. I am not the provider—God is (Jeremiah 29:11). God will not abandon me or forsake me (Hebrews 13:5).

Another lie is, *There are no more prospects.* The truth is that the harvest is plentiful, as Jesus says in Luke 10:2. Just as Jesus defeated Satan in the wilderness using God's Word (Luke 4:1–12), we must do the same in our own battle with Satan.

The second way we can control our thoughts is by writing down "whatever is honorable." We have all heard about the power of self-talk and self-affirmations. Yet many of us do not use this tool because it feels woo-woo and weird. At my low point in early 2020, however, I learned the power of writing down positive affirmations and then reviewing them each morning. This became part of my Rise and Go Manifesto.

One example of positive self-talk is that you may say, "I am a business leader who makes "$5k/month" (or "$50k/month"). You may say, "I am a great leader who equips and empowers the three people who report to me." (or maybe that number is 30, or 300.) Perhaps you'll say, "I am a high-performing doctor who provides great care to my patients," "I am a great parent," or "I am a devoted spouse."

Using "I am" statements will help you start to have more positive thoughts. The Law of Attraction states that positive thoughts bring positive results. This means that when you step into this mindset with boldness, you will increase the probability of what you envision coming true.

No matter how much money their companies earn or they themselves earn, all business leaders have negative thoughts that run through their minds. The difference between average leaders and great leaders is the speed at which they recalibrate and turn their negative thoughts into positive thoughts. Great leaders do not stay in the negative trenches quite as long as average leaders do. Great leaders still get knocked down. They just get up faster.

ACTION STEPS

Spend five minutes and list at least five negative thoughts that you have told yourself about your business or personal life. Spend another five minutes looking for Bible verses that offset those lies.

When you're done, write down ten "I am" statements that can help you rebuke those lies.

Here is an example of one of mine:

- A lie I sometimes tell myself: *I will not be successful with my coaching and speaking business because I was unsuccessful when I launched my real estate investment company.*
- A verse that has helped me: Romans 8:37, "No, in all these things we are more than conquerors through Him who loved us."
- The "I am" statement I use: *I am a conqueror and will overcome my present-day challenges and build this coaching and speaking business to impacts thousands of leaders!*

I encourage you to read your own statements out loud a few times a week to help you start your day in the right mental state and program your mind for success!

BONUS: RISE AND GO MANIFESTO

If you are like me, some of the lies and negative thoughts you have written down will reappear from time to time in your life. I encourage you to put your truth statements in your Rise and Go Manifesto in part 3, "I Am Statements." Reviewing these can remind you of the truth in your life and help you overcome these persistent lies.

PRAYER

Lord, I repent for having allowed negative thoughts to dominate my mind sometimes. Though I know you are in control, there are days when I feel doubt and fear that you have abandoned me. Lord, I pray that I will step into today with boldness and power to expand the Kingdom. I pray to think positively about my business, family members, coworkers, clients, and those I interact with today. Amen.

16

WHAT ARMOR ARE YOU PUTTING ON EACH DAY?

Leadership Trait: Preparedness

Ephesians 6:14, "Stand therefore, having fastened on the belt of truth, and having put on the breastplate of righteousness."

A couple years ago, my family attended a family camp where the theme was the "Armor of God." This term is taken from Ephesians 6:10–20. In this passage, Paul is telling the saints of Ephesus that there is a spiritual war going on and that we all need to armor up in order to defeat the enemy, which is Satan.

I was responsible for teaching about "the belt of truth" part of the armor, which is Jesus. The audience at this camp was made up of a mix of young kids and adults, and those of us on the event's leadership team decided that a skit would hold the attention of everyone in the room and be memorable.

As we began, I spread Legos out across the floor in the front of the conference room, in the shape of a large rectangle. These Legos represented the challenges and spiritual warfare attacks we all face in life.

I then had two volunteers walk across the Legos. The first was our "Armor of God" soldier, my friend Justin. Justin walked across the Legos with his hiking boots on because he was prepared with "the belt of truth." As you would expect, he was able to walk over them easily.

The second walker was my friend, Brad, who had to walk across the Legos without any shoes on! Let's just say that he did not make it very far across the Legos. He was grimacing and squealing very early on from the pain of the Legos against his bare feet. He eventually got down on his hands and knees, and finally asked if he could stop! Brad's painful walk represented what handling adversity and spiritual warfare attacks looks like when we don't have Jesus involved.

That is how life is! As we are building our business and family, we are going to come up against hard things, including spiritual warfare. How we respond to adversity and spiritual attacks will help determine the outcome.

There is a popular equation that business coach Tim Kight came up with that I use often with my clients. The equation is E + R = O. The idea of the equation is that an event (E) happens in our life and how we respond (R) will determine the outcome (O).

If we respond (R) well, then it is more than likely that we will experience the best possible outcome. If we don't respond well, we will more than likely face a bad outcome. This could in turn cause a ripple effect in other areas in our lives.

Recently my family experienced one of those twenty-four-hour time periods when not much went right. It started with me running downstairs to my office in the basement to get something. As I stepped onto my office carpet without my shoes on, I felt that it was soaked! We'd had a lot of rain recently, and the water had come up through the cracks in my office floor.

Not only was I mad about the water itself, but I was also wondering how I was going to repair the basement floor. I was further frustrated because now, in order to deal with the problem, I had to immediately remove everything from my office! As is usually the case when crises hit, this was not ideal timing because I had a very busy week ahead. The last thing I wanted to do was spend any time on office reconstruction.

Later that day, after working on the problem in my office for a few hours, I went outside to grill cheeseburgers for dinner. Now one of my favorite things to do on a nice day is grill and listen to music while having a beer and relaxing. However, when I went to turn on the garage speakers and music, our Wi-Fi was not working in the garage! So instead of music and relaxation, I got a lot more tension and aggravation.

I know, I know, these are all First World problems. I get it. But even First World problems can be incredibly frustrating.

The next day when I woke up and went downstairs, my daughter Kamdyn, twelve years old at the time, had left on the kitchen counter a piece of art she'd made. She wanted me to see it. It said: "Just Breathe, God is with you."

Seeing that piece of art was the first step in improving my outlook on life and getting me back in a productive mental state. To this day, it remains in my office as a reminder for me to slow down. Although this art was helpful, however, it didn't get me fully over the mental hump. The weight of the wet basement floor and the Wi-Fi that wasn't working still hung over me in a way that felt suffocating.

The final step in my mental breakthrough occurred after I decided to go up to Kiley's room, my then sixteen-year-old daughter, to check in on her and see how she was doing. Kiley had woken up with a very stiff neck. The pain was so bad that she had an appointment with the chiropractor scheduled for later that day.

While I was in her room, I decided to pray for her neck, and it was while I was praying for her that it hit me: all these recent events were a spiritual attack! The devil was trying to steal our joy because we had a lot of great things happening in our life, including a new car and new clients for my business. My son's basketball team had recently finished their season undefeated, we had just scheduled Kiley's first official college visit, and we had just received the good news that Kamdyn had received medical clearance after a hip injury to compete in all four events at an upcoming gymnastic meet!

So, yes, we had a lot of great things happening in our family. Once I realized the devil was trying to steal our joy, I immediately invited Jesus in to cast out the devil and any other negativity that was going on. Instantly, I felt better. I immediately sent a text to our family's text chain stating all the above, explaining that we needed to be aware of it as a family, and assuring them that we were going to overcome the funk we were in.

Yes, we still had to deal with some outcomes from the previous twenty-four hours. Kiley still had to see the chiropractor. I still had to clean up my wet office. However, how we responded with prayer and unity, changing the outcome instead of allowing ourselves to be pawns in the devil's game. By putting on the "belt of truth" and inviting Jesus into our situation, we were able to overcome it better than we would have if we'd gone at it alone.

Building a business and a family is hard work. Just when you start to get some joy and momentum in your life, the devil will try and knock you down. It may even work for a moment, as it did with our family. But you can turn things around by speaking against the devil and inviting Jesus into the situation.

When you invite Jesus into the stressful situations in your life, you will start to experience the kind of peace that is described in Philippians 4:7: "And the peace of God, which surpasses all understanding, will guard your hearts and your minds in Christ Jesus."

ACTION STEPS

Spend five minutes writing down places where you may be seeing spiritual warfare in your life.

- Where are you seeing resistance in your life, either at work or at home?
- Are there relationships that are not where they should be?
- Do you feel God speaking to your spirit that a relationship needs to be healed?
- What frustrating events are occurring in your life? Broken appliances, cracked windshields, computer breaking down, work travel logistics and coordination, etc.

Now spend five minutes writing down how you can invite Jesus into each of those situations and any newfound wisdom you have learned from God.

PRAYER

Lord, thank you for protecting me against the physical and spiritual attacks I see in my life. I know there are so many attacks that are happening that I don't even know about, so thanks for protecting me against those too. I realize that sometimes when I face attacks, I fail to turn to you. Instead I try to "pull myself up by my own bootstraps" and defeat the enemy on my own. Lord, I invite you in to help me in the battle against the devil. I pray that I will be quicker to fight and not withdraw. Quicker to pull you in, instead of doing things my way. Thank you for being by my side. Amen.

17

WHAT ARE YOU DISTRACTED BY?

Leadership Trait: Peace

Luke 10:40, "But Martha was distracted with much serving. And she went up to him and said, 'Lord, do you not care that my sister has left me to serve alone? Tell her then to help me.'"

In the story of Martha and Mary, Martha was busy doing dishes and cleaning the house—just focused on her tasks. Whereas Mary was at peace, having a still heart and mind, and she sat at Jesus's feet—just hanging out and being present with Him.

The reality described here probably sums up more than their current actions in this verse. I would venture to guess that these words reflect the states of mind the two women had most of the time.

Martha was probably always busy. In today's world, Martha would constantly be looking at her phone to see if she was needed by a customer or coworker. She would have a tough time taking vacation or cutting out of work a few hours early because she is "needed." She might say things like, "If I don't do it, it won't get done," and "Everybody is always asking for my help." Jesus even said to Martha in verse 41, "You are anxious and troubled about many things."

In contrast, Mary was calm. Yes, Mary still got her work done, but she could leave her work once she was finished. In today's world, Mary would not be tethered to her phone. She would not be weighed down by every single task. She knows she has a team who will help her. Mary also knows to spend her time on the tasks that matter and that make the greatest impact to her business and her life.

My hunch is that Mary would be a believer of the Pareto Principle, a concept that can help many of us. Used in the business world, the Pareto Principle, which was created by economist Vilfredo Pareto, states that 80 percent of consequences come from 20 percent of the causes. This means that, at least on some tasks, there is an unequal relationship between the efforts we put in and the results we see.

For example, in your business, 20 percent of your customers probably make up 80 percent of your revenue. This is not a law. It's more a common relationship between effort and results. We see this principle at work in our personal lives as well, where 80 percent of the positive output in our lives derives from 20 percent of our time. We spend a lot of time on meaningless tasks, such as scrolling social media, running errands, etc. Yet our greatest impact can come out of our solitude time, as well as from time spent with friends and family.

In Luke 10, Mary was living out the Pareto Principle. In her mind, washing dishes could wait for another time. Being with Jesus in that moment was much more critical. We can see a lot of ourselves when we look at Mary and Martha. Unfortunately, I am probably more Martha than I would like to admit.

Martha's posture says that moving fast and staying busy is

better than slowing down and being still. She seemed to live out the idea that *doing* is better than just *being*. There are many times when it can be hard for me to sit still and journal, pray, or read Scripture. When I start to do any of those activities, I begin to wonder if I should be sending out emails or doing some form of work instead. Yet I need to slow down and be in the moment with God. The emails can wait. We all need to slow down, so that we can speed up later!

When I am at my best, I am focused instead of distracted. I am present in the place where I am. If I am in the room with my family, then I am there to talk, listen, and hang out, and not look at the TV or my phone. When I am in quiet time, then I am reading the Scripture and praying instead of checking my computer or phone in between verses.

Those are examples of my good days when I am not distracted. However, the devil loves when we are distracted. That's because in those times, we are not as effective. We can't grow closer to God when we have a distracted quiet time. We can't develop deep relationships with others and listen well when we are not mentally present. I have heard it said before that the devil doesn't have to make us bad. He just has to make us busy!

Anytime in my life that I have experienced a breakthrough, it has happened because I put together enough focused moments to achieve that breakthrough. By contrast, I have never felt close to God when my quiet time is interrupted with distractions and notifications.

What about you? Are you overwhelmed because you are so distracted in your daily life that you are never just still? If we are not careful, the busyness of life can lead us to spend way too much time on activities that are not important in the grand scheme of things.

In Luke 10:42 Jesus says, "Mary has chosen the good portion, which will not be taken away from her." When we, like Mary, spend time with Jesus—when we invest in our quiet time—we grow in wisdom, become better rooted in our identity, and further build an intimate relationship with God that is permanent. Tasks, on the other hand, are temporary. It can be hard for me sometimes to even remember the last ten messages I sent, or the last three meetings I had. Often, this is because those activities were not life changing. Sometimes we just find ourselves spending our days running in the hamster wheel of tasks.

If we go about life like Martha, then we are never at an internal peace. We are constantly "doing" and thinking that we are in control of our life. Or we might be busy hustling because we're trying to win our boss's approval, or because we feel our identity is tied to that achievement. The error in this thinking is that it causes us to play God, instead of accepting that God is in charge.

Scan QR code to listen to the podcast

Ron Kitchens, author of *Uniquely You,* shared a story on my podcast that has stuck with me for months. During our interview, I asked Ron if there were any moments in his life when he had felt he needed to hand over his story for an even greater story. Meaning, did he ever feel that he had to hand over his life in order to do what God was calling him to do?

He then shared with me about a time when his family had a family reunion in South Padre Island. Although she was not wealthy, Ron's mother-in-law had saved enough money to rent a nice house where her kids and their families could all stay together. While everyone was spending time together and enjoying their vacation, however, Ron was working on a potential business deal.

In fact, Ron spent the entire vacation working on that business deal—only to come home and see it fall apart! This was the wakeup call that Ron needed. He had been on the hamster wheel of being busy, and he had been choosing work over family for years.

Ron felt a nudge from God to start managing his time better. And ever since that experience, Ron has been budgeting his time the way many of us budget our finances. Using a spreadsheet, Ron tracks how he spends his time with work, friends, family, self, and God.

To make sure he never falls back into his old habits, Ron even has the words "South Padre Island" in large font in the top right corner of the spreadsheet to remind him of his "why." He was done being distracted, and he was ready to focus on what he cared about most.

ACTION STEPS

Spend five minutes blocking out time in your calendar for a few critical activities that often get overlooked but that are crucial to the health of our lives and in our businesses:

- Quiet time: This is your time of solitude, during which you will pray and journal. Try to schedule at least four per week.
- Relationships: Schedule dates with your spouse, kids, and good friends. Try to have at least one date a month with your spouse.
- Exercise: This is time for you to work out by going to the gym, walking, or doing some other form of physical activity. Schedule at least three sessions per week.
- Think time: This is time set aside for you to strategize and think about your business. The amount of time can vary, based on an individual's needs, but schedule at least one hour per week.

BONUS

I encourage you to do a time audit of one or two days of your week. Many of us underestimate the amount of time we waste, and this activity helps to bring about awareness regarding areas for improvement. To do a time audit, write down what you do during every thirty-minute block of time and evaluate your findings at the end of the day.

After doing this for a couple of days, review the results and identify where you are spending quality time and where you are wasting time. Think about ways you can optimize your quality times and reduce your wasted time.

PRAYER

Lord, please forgive me for the times I have been too distracted to have quiet time. I am guilty of interrupting my quiet time, prayer life, and time with you because I am so busy "doing." I want to be more like Mary, who knew that there is a time to work and a time to sit at your feet. Amen.

18

WHAT ARE YOU HOLDING ON TO?

Leadership Trait: Commitment

2 Kings 13:18, "And he said, 'Take the arrows,' and he took them. And he said to the king of Israel, 'Strike the ground with them.' And he struck three times and stopped."

As I mentioned earlier in the book, when I was terminated from my executive job in corporate America over five years ago, I was given a four-month severance package. At the time, I viewed my termination and severance package as a nudge from God to go after my dream of having a coaching and speaking career.

Over the next couple of years and through God's provision, I was able to build the coaching and speaking business to the point that I knew this was what I wanted to do for a living. I could also see that my new business would provide financially for my family. There was no denying that God's hands were all over my transition from corporate America to full-time coaching and speaking, because I clearly saw Him orchestrating the opportunities and relationships that were allowing me to build my business.

Yet even though I was well aware of God's involvement in this transition, I still could not bring myself to let go of the ongoing process of renewing my professional engineering license, which allowed me to practice Civil Engineering. I'd had the license for a long time—since four years after graduating from the University of Missouri with a Civil Engineering degree, in fact. Over the next sixteen years in my corporate career, the license was a vital qualification that allowed me to work in key executive roles in corporate America. For example, my most recent corporate job was as President of Sales for a specialty construction contractor, and my name had been listed as the corporate registered engineer for many project bids and submittals.

As with other professional licenses, I had to maintain professional development hours and submit the paperwork every two years stating that I had completed my professional development hours. For a period of time, I continued to do this after I'd launched my coaching and speaking business, even though I no longer needed this license in my daily work.

Why was it so hard for me to release my professional engineering license? Was I planning to go back to the engineering field and to corporate America? Was that my "Plan B" if coaching didn't work out?

All that changed a couple of years ago. When the time came for me to renew my license again, I happened to be reading a book by Erwin McManus, who is lead pastor of Mosaic, a megachurch in California, and has written some of my favorite Christian books. The book I was reading was, *The Last Arrow*. Now, I always enjoy Erwin's teachings, both those in his books and his sermons. Yet I was not anticipating the breakthrough I had with this book.

The Last Arrow is based on a biblical story in 2 Kings 13:14–19. In this story Joash, King of Israel, was stressed about an upcoming battle, so he asked the Prophet Elisha for help. Elisha directed King

Joash to get his bow and quiver of arrows. Once King Joash did that, Elisha told him to take one arrow out of the quiver and shoot it eastward out the window. King Joash did as he was instructed.

Next, Elisha said, "The Lord's arrow of victory, the arrow of victory over Syria! For you shall fight the Syrians in Aphek until you have made an end of them" (verse 17). Basically, Elisha was stating that because King Joash had shot the Lord's arrow, his army would defeat Syria.

Elisha then ordered King Joash to "take the arrows" (verse 18) out of his quiver and "strike the ground with them" (verse 18). This time, however, King Joash only went partway. He only shot three arrows into the ground, keeping the remaining arrows in his quiver!

Instantly Elisha scolded the king. Verse 19 says, "Then the man of God was angry with him and said, 'You should have struck five or six times; then you would have struck down Syria until you had made an end of it, but now you will strike down Syria only three times.'"

As Elisha predicted, King Joash went on to defeat Syria only three times. This was not enough to win the war, so instead of defeating their enemy, his army was eventually overcome by Syria.

So why didn't King Joash shoot all the arrows?

For the same reason we don't. King Joash probably kept some arrows in his quiver so he'd have them if God didn't show up and he needed to finish the work himself. We, too, tend to keep some arrows in our quiver because we think God may forget about us.

MY LAST ARROW

As I was processing *The Last Arrow*, the issue of my professional license renewal kept coming to mind as an arrow in my quiver. As I dug in deeper, I realized that I was holding on to my license in case I decided to give up on my entrepreneurial journey of coaching.

I knew God had called me into coaching. But I was holding on to my license just in case God didn't show up at some point. The reality is, leaving my corporate job and pursuing the coaching path had been an amazing experience, but it was also a stressful one. I felt the burden of being the financial provider for my wife and three kids. Plus, the constant pressure of doing ongoing business development, creating new content, and constantly being on the lookout for ways to bring value to leaders can be exhausting some days.

One irony of my job is that success means that I help get clients unstuck. This means that they eventually will fire me because they no longer need me! This client rotation causes some volatility in income from month to month. This was especially true when I was beginning to build my business, which made things extra challenging and stressful.

Whenever times got tough in the coaching business, I would wonder *what if*. What if I called someone in my old network and got a job? What if I stopped trying to build something on my own and joined a corporation that already had momentum instead? What if I were to trade in the financial ebb and flow of coaching engagements for a consistent salary provided by a company? As I was reading *The Last Arrow*, I realized that I needed to cut bait with my professional engineering license because it was becoming my last arrow in my quiver.

I had shot one of the Lord's arrows out the window when I left my corporate career for coaching. Now I needed to shoot out *all* my arrows in my quiver, just as Elisha had directed King Joash to do. I knew that there would be plenty of hard days ahead, and there were. There still are, to this day. But God had shown me that every day I am being called up and equipped to go after this profession.

And so, after processing these insights through prayer, journaling, and conversations with my mentors, I decided to allow my professional engineering license to expire. I shot my last arrow!

Shooting the last arrow in our quiver is a step we need to take so that God will take *His* next step. Bryan Kaiser, founding partner and Chief Business Development Officer of the staffing and recruitment company Vernovis, shared with me on my podcast "Win at Home First," the idea that God is the best chess player ever. What did Bryan mean by this? "He will wait for us to make the move."

Scan QR code to listen to the podcast

God wants to be in relationship with us as we go about our lives. But He also wants us to take steps of obedience. God just didn't simply part the Red Sea when Moses and the Israelites walked up to it. Instead, God wanted Moses to make the first move. He told him: "Lift up your staff, and stretch out your hand over the sea and divide it, that the people of Israel may go through the sea on dry ground" (Exodus 14:16).

God wanted Moses to demonstrate his faith in God by making a move.

We see a similar situation when Joshua was leading the Israelites across the Jordan. The Lord told Joshua: "When you come to the brink of the waters of the Jordan, you shall stand still in the Jordan" (Joshua 3:8). Once the Israelites made the move to stand in the water and have faith in God, then God parted the Jordan River (3:15–16).

We need to release the arrow in our quiver because doing so is a demonstration of our faith. It is another sign to God that we are committed to His call to follow Him.

I also believe that there is great freedom to be found in shooting those last arrows when the time is right. After I allowed my license to expire, I knew at last that I was "all-in" with coaching. Once that happened, I started showing up to work differently, with new excitement and vigor that equipped me to build my new business with courage instead of timidity.

ACTION STEPS

Spend five minutes thinking about the goals and dreams you are pursuing. Consider the following questions:

- What is the last arrow in your quiver?
- Are you holding on to a backup plan?
- Is there a mindset you need to release?
- An identity change you need to make?
- Are there actions or thoughts you need to stop or reduce in order to pursue your next step?

It is okay to have a backup plan in the beginning when you're starting something new. But there is also a time to a shoot the last arrow. This exercise is about helping you figure out whether now is the time for you to shoot your last arrow.

PRAYER

Lord, thank you for great stories in the Bible that help us realize we are not alone with our doubts and that provide great metaphors for us to reflect on our own lives. Please help me to see what I may be holding on to now. Is there an arrow in my quiver that I don't know about? Please make me aware of any places in my life where I am playing it safe and holding on to something. I want to live in freedom, instead of tethered to safety. Amen.

19

WHAT IS GOD CALLING YOU TO DO?

Leadership Trait: Obedience

Acts 9:11, "And the Lord said to him, 'Rise and go to the street called Straight, and at the house of Judas look for a man of Tarsus named Saul, for behold he is praying.'"

One of the most famous Bible stories is the conversion of Saul, who was one of the most outspoken leaders *against* Jesus before he became Paul, one of the most outspoken leaders *for* Jesus. But before this transition could take place, another man named Ananias had to be obedient to God.

At the beginning of Acts 9, Saul was on his way to Damascus to capture and kill followers of Jesus. But while he was on his way, a sudden light from heaven caused Saul to fall to the ground (Acts 9:3–4).

At that moment, Jesus asked him, "Saul, Saul, why are you persecuting me?" (Acts 9:4). Jesus then told Saul to go and enter the city of Damascus, where he would receive further instructions. Saul, now blind from this encounter, was led to Damascus by his traveling companions. For three days Saul remained without sight while he waited to learn what would happen next.

Meanwhile, Ananias, a disciple in Damascus, received a vision that is described in Acts 9:11–12. He was told to "rise and go to the street called Straight, and at the house of Judas look for a man of Tarsus named Saul, for behold, he is praying, and he has seen in a vision a man named Ananias come in and lay his hands on him so that he might regain his sight."

Knowing all the evil that Saul had done, Ananias pushed back with the Lord on this seemingly crazy idea. But the Lord said to Ananias, "Go, for he is a chosen instrument of mine to carry my name before the Gentiles and kings and the children of Israel" (Acts 9:15).

Imagine how crazy this would feel if it happened in your life! Think of some of the evil people in time who embarked on missions to have large numbers of people murdered, such as Hitler. What if you were told to go speak and pray over him? I know I would be scared and reluctant. Though our situations are not nearly that extreme, we often resist when God prompts us to go pray over a neighbor, a friend, or a family member. Even that task can be scary and daunting for many of us!

Even though Ananias was reluctant, however, he was obedient and went to meet Saul. Ananias did as commanded and laid his hand on Saul and prayed for him to "regain your sight and be filled with the Holy Spirit" (Acts 9:17).

Verse 18 tells us, "And immediately something like scales fell from his eyes, and he regained his sight. Then he rose and was baptized." At that moment, a conversion occurred in Saul's heart. He was no longer against Jesus, but *for* Jesus. This marked the beginning of Saul's, soon to be Paul's, ministry. And this ministry was a significant one, as he went on to spread the gospel widely and wrote thirteen of the twenty-seven books that are in the New

Testament! Ananias would not have had the opportunity to be part of this transition from Saul to Paul if he had not said "yes" to rise and go.

HEARING FROM GOD

When was the last time you heard God telling you to go and do something? Before we proceed, it is probably a good idea to establish what hearing from God is and how often it happens to people. When I hear other people's stories about how they heard from God, I can sometimes get the feeling that God is not talking to me at all, but that He is talking to others every step of the way. When I get these thoughts, I feel defeated and discouraged.

But hearing from God can take a lot of different forms. God might speak to you in a dream or a vision, as He did with Ananias. You might hear from Him through a timely word delivered by a trusted advisor or wise counselor in your life. Maybe, instead, during a time of prayer you feel a sense of peace or a new level of confidence concerning the next step you can take on an issue you have been praying about. Sometimes for me, a word or phrase can seem to jump off the page while I am reading Scripture.

As for frequency, I can't say how often God speaks to others. I just know that in my own life, I hear from God less frequently when I am not spending time with Him. When I am too busy with work or social media, or when I have too much noise going on in my life, then I don't make space to hear His voice, which can often come as "the sound of a low whisper" (1 Kings 19:12). I know that when I need to hear from God, I need to slow down and spend more time with Him. Praying, spending time in solitude, reading Scripture, and listening to worship music all help me to do this.

Scan QR code to listen to the podcast

Dan Britton, Chief Field Officer at Fellowship of Christian Athletes (FCA), shared on my podcast that he uses the term "linger longer" to refer to what we must do to hear from God. When we are in our quiet time, instead of just quickly reading the verse of the day, we should in fact *linger longer* to see if we hear anything from God in that moment.

It is when we do, in fact, slow down that we can hear from God.

The phrase "rise and go," which served as the inspiration for this book's title, is all about rising up from when we feel knocked down or when we're just busy doing our normal activities, but then changing direction to go do whatever different thing God is calling us to do that day. This is exactly what Ananias did. In Acts 22:12, Paul describes Ananias to a crowd in Jerusalem as "a devout man according to the law, well spoken of by all the Jews who lived there." A man this honorable would not have been sitting around doing nothing in the moment that God spoke to him. He would have had a day filled with good and valuable activities ahead of him.

Still, God called him to "rise and go"—to stop what he was doing, even though it was good, and to go and serve Saul instead. *Rise and go* is about being obedient to what God is calling us to do. Perhaps you, too, have had the experience of hearing God tell you to stop the good you are doing now, and to go and do something godly that serves somebody else instead. Maybe you felt a nudge to talk to somebody about a difficult situation? To apologize to your spouse for ways you have been acting? To spend time with one of your kids? To spend some time with a co-worker who is experiencing a challenging season?

One example from my own life is particularly vivid in my memory. This happened about eight years ago, when I was product manager of a multimillion-dollar product. At the time, I was working on a potential partnership with our biggest competitor that would have allowed my company to provide our customers with a solution we did not currently have in our portfolio. I had been going back and forth on the matter with our executive team, as well as the competitor, and it seemed as if the deal was about to die.

At that point Vern, who was not my direct boss at the time and would have benefited only minimally if this partnership succeeded, saw me in the hallway around lunch time. Seeing that I looked discouraged, he offered to help me out. Perhaps Vern was responding to a nudge like the one I've described. Getting just five minutes of his time would have been a huge win for me, due to his business acumen. However, I got a lot more than five minutes.

Vern started helping me around noon. It was the day before Thanksgiving, so the office was starting to clear out, and at 2 p.m. the CEO sent an email allowing everyone to leave early. I asked Vern if he wanted to stop, but he declined. He said he wanted to finish what we were working on!

Around 4 p.m. he got a call from his wife, asking when he would be home. I overheard him say, "One or two more hours. I want to help Cory with his partnership."

When we finally wrapped up at 6 p.m., I walked away with an outline of the partnership, an Excel spreadsheet showing revenue and margin scenarios, a modified contract, and a PowerPoint presentation ready to show the executive team!

The work Vern and I did that day ultimately saved the partnership. It contributed significantly to the growth of the product line involved. And quite honestly, it was a tipping point in my career.

I am confident that the partnership would not have been saved if Vern had not volunteered his time to help me. We never talked about why he had wanted to help me. But I am convinced that such nudges often come from God. And when those nudges come, I want to be ready to act.

WHAT IF WE ARE NOT HEARING ANYTHING FROM GOD?

It is worth discussing the fact that there are the periods when we simply don't feel that we are hearing from God! What do we do then? I know that when I am not hearing from God, I can almost become paralyzed. I don't feel sure of how to move forward. Do I go left, or do I go right? Sometimes this uncertainty causes me to not move at all.

My friend Ryan Berg, who is cofounder and Executive Director of Aruna, a non-profit for which I have privilege to be on the Board of Directors, which provides employment to women who have been freed from sex trafficking in India. Ryan is a friend and one of my spiritual mentors, and he shared a metaphor that I have found to be helpful when I am expecting God to tell me my every single move. Ryan says it's as if we go to God and ask Him, "Can I play in the backyard?" God says, "Yes, go play in the backyard, but don't go beyond the fence. I will be in the backyard, so we can be together."

Before we go play, we ask God, "Okay, but can I play in the sandbox, in the backyard?" God smiles, "Yes, do whatever fills you up and is good for the backyard."

We then say, "Thanks, but can I play with the blue bucket, in the sandbox, in the backyard?" God says, "Yes, the backyard is mine and all that is in it."

Just before running outside, we ask, "God, can I play with the red shovel and the blue bucket, in the sandbox, in the backyard?

This illustration seems comical when we're viewing it from the perspective of an outside observer. However, we often can be that little kid.

Yes, there are times we hear from God, and when we have an

opportunity to "rise and go" and obey God's direction. But there are other times—maybe many days, weeks, or even years—when we don't hear from God. In those times, we can't allow ourselves to become paralyzed. We must instead move forward in confidence, knowing that what Isaiah 30:21 says is true, even when we do get off track: "And your ears shall hear a word behind you, saying, 'This is the way, walk in it,' when you turn to the right or when you turn to the left." What is important is not whether we hear a clear word from God. What is important is that we walk with Him.

ACTION STEPS

Throughout this book you have been working to hear from God, and you are now taking action when you do! Well done! However, God is always at work, even when we don't hear a clear message from Him, and He is always interested in us joining in on the work.

Spend five minutes in quiet time listening for God to see if He is calling you to anything today. When you are done, write down anything you heard. Did you hear any promptings about where to take action in your life? These could be big ideas or small ones. They may be home, work, or community related. Determine a next action step you can take for anything that comes to mind and schedule when you will do it.

PRAYER

Lord, thank you for all you do. Thanks for putting wise leaders in my life. I repent for when I have not been aware of the needs of those around me. I also repent for the times I ignored promptings to help others because the effort would take too much time or cost too much money. I want to be more of a giver. I want to be used by you to help catapult other leaders into greatness. Amen.

20

WHO CAN YOU ENCOURAGE TODAY?

Leadership Trait: Encouragement

Romans 15:2, "Let each of us please his neighbor for his good, to build him up."

A couple of years ago, David Novak, who is the cofounder and retired chairman of Yum! Brands (owner of Pizza Hut, Taco Bell, and KFC), wrote an article for NBC News titled, "Here's the No. 1 Reason Why Employees Quit Their Jobs."[14] In this article, David claimed that the number one reason people leave their employers is a lack of recognition in the workplace. He went as far as calling the time we live in a time of "global recognition deficit."

David is also cofounder and CEO of oGoLead, a digital leadership platform that conducted a national research effort to quantify

---

14   David Novack, "Here's the No. 1 Reason Why Employees Quit Their Jobs," NBC News, June 21, 2019, https://www.nbcnews.com/better/lifestyle/here-s-no-1-reason-why-employees-quit-their-jobs-ncna1020031.

this phenomenon. The same NBC News article reports that they found that "82 percent of employees feel their supervisor doesn't recognize them for what they do." David went on to list a few barriers to recognizing employees that his team identified. The one that I see most commonly in my business is a lack of time.

Leaders are so busy with their long to-do lists and numerous pressing deadlines that they often don't see the value in stopping what they are doing to acknowledge and encourage their team. However, as David points out, "The time bosses spend on recognition is one of the best investments they can make." That's not just true in the workplace. Whatever role we're serving in—be it boss, parent, or friend—we must make time to recognize and encourage those we lead.

Now you may be thinking, "But Cory, I thought this was a book to get *me* fired up. To lift *me* up, not others. Cory, I am tired. It has been a hard couple of years. *I* need to be lifted up."

I know. I know.

That's one of the reasons I'm giving you this advice. I do believe that God commands us to encourage others, and that this encouragement is intended to benefit them. But I know, too, that when I encourage others, I also get filled up in the process.

Sometimes, when we are weak in a particular area, our best move is to give to others in exactly that area. And doing so causes us to grow.

For example, when someone is stingy with their money, acting generously can stretch them and be extremely rewarding. Though I still need to grow more, I personally grew in this area over the last year. Every year, I choose a word that will be my word of the year. I took this idea from the book *One Word that Will Change Your Life* by Jon Gordon, Dan Britton, and Jimmy Page. For 2021, I chose the word *give*. Because it was my word for the year, I kept the word at the forefront of my mind. As a result, there were numerous times when I found myself having a giving spirit. This took the form of simple acts like buying a meal for a friend or donating spontaneously to a cause.

It's easy to see that when someone has become self-absorbed, getting them to think about others can change their perspective on life in powerful ways. One example of this is that when negative people start to track three daily wins in their own lives, they start to change their mindset and adopt a more positive outlook.

The truth is, you may be feeling rather low. But if you live out the call of Romans 15:2 to "let each of us please his neighbor for his good, to build him up," your efforts won't just benefit others. They'll raise you up too.

In order to see this verse in all its power, we need to look at the verses that come before and after it. Romans 15:1 says, "We who are strong have an obligation to bear with the failings of the weak, and not to please ourselves."

What does that mean? In these verses, Paul was speaking to Christians and categorizing them into two groups: weak and strong. The weak Christians were the more legalistic Christians who believed they needed to live out the law of the Old Testament: following rules about eating certain meats, observing certain holidays, etc. The strong Christians, on the other hand, were the ones who believed that Jesus, through His death and resurrection, had satisfied the requirements of the law. This meant that they were not obligated to observe certain food restrictions or holidays.

We who are reading this now, who believe that Jesus is the Messiah and that He fulfilled the law of the Old Testament, are among the strong that Paul was referring to. Because of Jesus, we have a faith for what is and a hope for what is to come. This allows us to operate from a position of strength. As a result, we can build others up. We need to build up our families, our work teams, and our friends. And as we build up other people, we inevitably will be built up too.

Romans 15:4 tells us that the way we get filled up is "through endurance and through the encouragement of the Scriptures we might have hope." The message is very clear: Spending time with

God in Scripture is what fills us up. Seeing the biblical heroes and the battles that they went through and how they won gives us hope. Seeing the underdog win gives us hope. Knowing that Jesus will return gives us hope. If we are to grow and be the light, we must encourage others and we must spend time in the Word.

The flow of knowledge, such as the knowledge we get from Scripture, can be like a river or it can be like a reservoir. As tributaries feed into a river, it becomes more powerful as it flows downstream. In much the same way, when we share our growth and learning, our interactions with others become more valuable to them.

Whereas a reservoir with no input or outlet becomes stagnant water. It is simply still. This reminds me of times in my life when I became complacent and stopped spending time in the Bible. When that happened, I no longer had fresh information or insights to share with my clients, I heard God's voice less, and my words began to get stale.

If we want to provide timely and pinpointed encouragement, we need to be spending time in the Word and in prayer. This helps us to become more aware of others and their needs, and it equips us to provide the encouragement they need to hear.

We need to be filling ourselves up so much that our overflow can bless others.

I find it interesting that some of my more popular posts on LinkedIn are those in which I share Bible verses (including many I have explored in this book) and then make myself vulnerable by sharing my own doubts and insecurities. These comments resonate with leaders because they find encouragement in hearing about another person's struggles—as well as what got me through those hard times. I get encouragement from their comments made to the post itself, or when they reach out and privately message me to let me know how this post has impacted and encouraged them!

Through the process of encouraging others, we ourselves become encouraged.

Mike Hopkins, COO of Paul Davis Restoration, sees this play out in his company every day. Paul Davis Restoration has over 325 franchises throughout North America. These businesses restore residential and commercial properties after damage has been done by fire, water, or some other source.

Scan QR code to listen to the podcast

In my podcast conversation with Mike a little over a year ago, he said, "The best way to breathe life into someone is to catch them doing something good." He went on to say that finding ways to breathe life into others has become one of his favorite parts of his job. Why? Because it encourages him and fills his cup up!

He accomplishes this by looking for ways to celebrate and encourage his employees across the company. He has also enlisted his leadership team in the effort to encourage others, and this builds them up as well. At Mike's direction, the company's franchise owners, regional business consultants, and VPs are on the lookout for people who are doing good. When they see something positive happening, they provide Mike the name and contact information for the person involved, along with the story of what that person did that was good.

Mike then uses this information to encourage the company's workers. He does this by calling two to three employees per week throughout the organization, in locations all over North America, to tell them "Thank you."

Encouragement isn't just good for the people who receive it and give it. Mike likes to say, "What gets celebrated, gets accelerated."

One practical result of this truth is that when we build up people, our businesses grow as well.

ACTION STEPS

Spend five minutes praying for people in your life: family, friends, and coworkers. Does anyone come to mind as a person who may need some extra encouragement? Sometimes God places people on our mind for a reason. If someone popped into your mind, find a way to encourage that individual today, or as soon as you can. If no one individual came to mind, then just pick anyone you'd like. It never hurts to encourage a family member or a coworker!

PRAYER

Lord, I pray that your Word will give me the strength I need to invest in other people. I repent of the times I've failed to encourage others because I was preoccupied by my own little world and worried about my own problems. Lord, I pray for eyes to see those around me who need to be encouraged, and I ask you to give me the words to encourage them. Amen.

21

HOW DO YOU HANDLE DIFFICULT CHALLENGES?

Leadership Trait: Perseverance

Mark 1:25, "But Jesus rebuked him, saying, "Be silent, and come out of him!"

A few years ago, Holly and I traveled to Napa Valley, California, for our twentieth wedding anniversary. We were excited about this trip and thankful to be able to celebrate twenty years of marriage, three awesome kids, and the countless adventures we'd experienced while living in three different cities.

Together we have journeyed through a handful of different jobs we both had, plus my new entrepreneurial path of being a coach, author, and speaker. Our marriage has also survived many ups and downs, including a near bankruptcy and an affair I had, two subjects I address in more depth in my first book, *Win at Home First*.

Despite these hardships, we were still together, and we were grateful for that fact. It is an understatement to say that we had a lot to celebrate on this trip!

However, our anniversary trip didn't start off perfectly. The plan was to land at the San Francisco airport, eat lunch at a recommended downtown restaurant, and then drive to Napa for our first wine tasting reservation. We knew it would be a tight schedule but manageable. But from the time we landed, everything started to take longer than our itinerary had room for. Our flight landed a little later than planned, and then we had to wait in a long car rental line. As we got in the rental car and drove to downtown, the internal stress was starting to build in each of us, and we were quickly reminded of how the devil comes to "steal, kill, and destroy" our joy and happiness (John 10:10).

As you are probably aware, San Francisco traffic in the morning can be very heavy. To make matters worse, as we are driving into downtown, both of us becoming more and more internally stressed that our schedule was getting off track, I missed a very important exit. It was one of those massive interstate exchanges where multiple highways come together, so if you miss an exit, you must drive a couple of miles out of the way to get an exit option to turn around. Let's just say, when I was finally able to turn around, we were going in the direction headed into the city that was bumper-to-bumper traffic!

By the time we arrived at our highly anticipated restaurant, it was an hour and half wait for lunch! We did not have time for a long lunch, but more importantly, we were both starting to get "hangry"—angry from being hungry! So we settled for another place for lunch.

I don't know if the devil can cause us to miss our highway exits. But I do know that he can cause our emotions and reactions to flare up. As we drove toward Napa with a high probability of missing our first wine tasting reservation, we were not the same couple who had eagerly packed for this trip just a few days earlier.

Maybe it was the early morning flight, the bad traffic, or my dumb mistake of missing the exit. I was sure Holly was mad at me. I was certainly mad at myself. I was in such a bad mood that I no longer wanted to talk with her. The few times I did talk, it was only about how our trip was off to a bad start.

After about ten minutes of this stressful drive, Holly called the situation out, saying, "The devil is trying to ruin our twentieth anniversary." Yes, that was it! The devil was trying to steal our joy by making us mad and shifting our attention from our big celebration to some small, unpleasant, and temporary inconveniences.

Right then and there, while we were still driving, we prayed off this spiritual warfare attack. Almost immediately, the tension, anger, and dark mood in the car lifted. We were back to ourselves and back to celebrating our marriage!

Throughout the next few days, as we celebrated, we talked about our rough first day. At times we laughed about it and other times we did get annoyed about it. However, we no longer got angry or felt frustrated with each other. Instead, we felt clear that we were in this together.

Jesus shows us how to handle these spiritual warfare situations in Mark 1. The beginning of the chapter tells of Jesus being baptized by John the Baptist, and then God immediately affirmed Him. As Jesus came up out of the water, God said, "You are my beloved Son, with you I am well pleased" (Mark 1:11).

At that point in Scripture, Jesus began His mission of sharing the Good News with others. Later, Jesus was teaching in the synagogue. While He was teaching, a demon-possessed man came in and caused havoc. This man yelled at Jesus, called Him a fraud, and caused a scene. But Jesus did not get discouraged and stop. Instead, He acted as if He expected the distraction.

Jesus did not debate, converse, or even try to plead with the evil spirit. Jesus firmly said, "Be silent, and come out of him" (Mark 1:25), and then He continued teaching.

We need to do the same thing in our own lives!

EXPECT RESISTANCE

As you are pressing toward your goals, know that you will face resistance. Know that the devil will try to knock you backwards. Instead of being discouraged, be expectant, brush it off, and move on.

Resistance shows up in all areas of our lives, both personal and professional. You may want to start working out and going to the gym. But the night before, the devil challenges your self-control, tempting you with food and drink. The result is that the next morning, you don't want to get up early and go to the gym. Or perhaps at work you are building momentum, so the devil introduces jealousy or strife into the team, causing friction and tension.

Spiritual warfare is real, and I encourage you to be aware of it. Now we can't blame every problem on spiritual warfare. All of us have made our fair share of stupid decisions and poor choices where we have no one to blame but ourselves. However, we can't be in denial about its existence either.

Holly and I experienced breakthrough in our marriage once we learned about spiritual warfare and acknowledged its existence. For example, it is almost inevitable that when I go out of town—especially for a faith-rich experience, such as my men's group's trip to Florida or the mission trip to Nicaragua—something bad will happen at home.

When Kiley and I went to Nicaragua, Holly had an awful experience with vertigo that had her sick on the floor, and neighbors had to come over to take care of her. When I went to Florida with my small group, Holly had an awful night due to food poisoning. Another time, when I took a trip to Montana as part of a men's ministry, our washing machine broke.

All these things may have happened even if I hadn't traveled. However, the timing is very interesting! Before Holly and I knew about spiritual warfare, we would have been frustrated with each other. She might have felt mad that I was on a great trip, and I might have felt upset because her plight was distracting me from my spiritual opportunities.

Now, though, we call out spiritual warfare and use it to unite us. We realize that, as Paul says in Ephesian 6:12, "We do not wrestle against flesh and blood, but against the rulers, against the authorities, against the cosmic powers over this present darkness, against the spiritual forces of evil in the heavenly places."

The next time you feel that you and your spouse are out of sync and headed down an argumentative path, I encourage you to call it out. Pray off the spiritual warfare. Don't just try to brush it under the carpet and ignore it. That might work in the moment, but tension only builds, and the battle only grows stronger when we don't address our challenges head on.

Whenever you notice spiritual warfare attacks in your professional life, pray those off as well. Depending on the office dynamics in your workplace, you may or may not be able to pray with your team. But I encourage you to at least pray individually against the spiritual warfare that you are facing at work.

No matter where spiritual attacks occur in your life, keep persevering. That is the path to spiritual victory, to peace, and to elevating our mindset.

ACTION STEPS

Spend five minutes praying about the pain, suffering, and negativity you are experiencing in your life, whether that pain is occurring in your marriage, at work, or just in your mind. Be honest with God and lay out for Him just where your frustrations lie.

Next, spend time inviting God into these situations to help you.

Finally, rebuke the negative emotions and bad situations, and ask God to give you wisdom and show you the path to overcoming your situation.

PRAYER

Lord, thank you for this verse and Your example of how to handle spiritual warfare. I repent of all the times I've let myself get knocked down and have become discouraged too easily. I am encouraged by this verse to brush those experiences off and move on. I pray for strength to brush them off more quickly than normal! Amen.

22

WHAT IS THE NEXT STEP YOU CAN TAKE?

Leadership Trait: Consistency

Exodus 23:30, "Little by little I will drive them out from before you, until you have increased and possess the land."

In the passages that lead up to this verse in Exodus, God tells Moses about the Ten Commandments and the other laws of the covenant. Then God tells Moses that, now that the Israelites know the laws, if they obey them He will lead them to conquer their enemies and give them land that stretches "from the Red Sea to the Mediterranean Sea and from the Wilderness to the Euphrates River" (Exodus 23:31 The Message).

In the previous verse God told Moses that He would go before Israel "little by little" to help them conquer the land and their enemies that occupy it. I believe the message of this verse applies just as fully to you and me. God is at work now for us, just like

He was with Moses. And so I believe He also goes before us "little by little."

Some days I am okay with the words "little by little," while other days I find them annoying. Some days, I just don't have time for baby steps.

I want customers to line up to get my services.

I want to launch a new program for my business, such as a month-long challenge, and I want tons of people show up for it.

I want to give my kids responsibility, and I don't want to have to tell them to do something more than once. I especially don't want to have to tell them to do every step of the process. I want them to learn a few steps and then go off to do the rest on their own!

Deep down, sometimes I just want to take the easy path.

I get myself into trouble by wanting not "little by little" but "big by big." Or—even better—"enormous by enormous."

Everyone wants to be an overnight success. But the truth is, there is no such thing. Even famous YouTube gamers played for thousands of hours in their basements before they were discovered. Popular TikTok dancers logged thousands of hours dancing in their bedrooms before they were discovered. Successful musicians wrote hundreds of songs before you ever heard their hit songs. Even top sales leaders held numerous meetings with prospects before they landed their clients.

In his 2008 bestseller *Outliers*, author and journalist Malcom Gladwell describes the science behind the idea that practice makes perfect. Malcom's thesis in the book is that a person will achieve mastery in a particular skill after practicing that skill for 10,000 hours. Of course, no one can put in 10,000 hours in a day, or a week, or a month. Getting to 10,000 hours happens little by little.

Meanwhile, as we're putting in our hours, the devil is telling us there are overnight successes all around us and other people are achieving mastery faster than we are. Why does the devil do this? Because this idea deflates and discourages every one of us.

Once we become discouraged enough, then we quit.

When we quit, the devil wins.

But when we persist, adjust, and keep going, then the devil loses. We win the battle. But we aren't doing the work on our own. While you and I are doing the work of persisting, God is going before us to pave the way for our lives and businesses.

WHY "LITTLE BY LITTLE"?

It makes sense that advancing "little by little" eventually brings results. But many of us still wonder why mastery must be achieved in this way. It's a question worth asking. In fact, I believe that if we understand why God designed things to work this way, we can better appreciate the process and so have more patience and grace for those terms, and for ourselves.

In the English Standard Version translation of Exodus 23:30, God told Moses that He would drive the enemy out "until you have increased and possess the land." The Message version describes it even more fully, "Little by little I'll get them out of there while you have a chance to get your crops going and make the land your own."

Having more time helps us to prepare ourselves. We see this today, just as the Israelites surely did. If we grow too fast, our companies will break. We will break.

Yes, we want the quick spike in revenue. Yes, we wish to be an overnight success. But if we don't have processes in place that will allow us to handle all the new customers we get, then we will disappoint those customers—and we will have to do a lot of damage control. The "little by little" approach allows us to put infrastructure in place so we will be able to handle the uptick in activity.

I believe God's "little by little" was intentional and that He still uses it today because He loves us. He wants us to take one step at a time so we don't fail. I do this with my own kids. I want to give them responsibility gradually, so they don't get overwhelmed by sudden responsibility and then fail.

For example, years ago when I wanted my older daughter to babysit my younger kids, we set it up through a progression of steps. The first time, we had her watch them for an hour and did not ask her to do any feeding or meal prep. When that was successful, the next time we increased the length of time and had her make lunch for them as well. When this was successful, we continued to add more time and responsibility.

By contrast, if my daughter's very first babysitting experience had consisted of watching her sister and brother for a full day, preparing three meals, and doing the laundry, then the experience would have been a disaster. The demands would have been so overwhelming and stressful that Holly and I probably would have come home to find the house a mess, the oven still turned on, dishes piled in the sink, and our kids having temper tantrums and arguments.

Because I love my kids, I don't want to set them up to fail. I want to help equip and empower them by having them take on responsibility in small steps. I believe that God does the same thing, going before us and preparing the way, little by little. I think He softens the hearts of the right customers for us to talk to, as well as the hearts of our spouse or friends when a difficult conversation needs to happen. He gives us unique ideas that will help us grow our businesses and organizations—not all at once, but just in time, as we need them.

Although this is not just about business. This is also about our personal lives. We need to make sure we are growing little by little in all areas of development. Our capacity as business leaders grows as both our character and our competency in life grow. The more responsibilities we hold at home and work, the more diligent we must be about making sure our character is growing and remaining strong.

Each choice we make takes us closer or further away from our desired goal, little by little. If we pile up enough bad choices, then we end up way off the mark, regardless of our good intentions. Such bad choices might include an addiction, an affair, weight gain, or unethical business practices. The scary reality is, these mistakes all start off with one small bad move that leads to another, and then another. On the other hand, if we consistently make good choices, then little by little, we align ourselves with a greater outcome.

LOOK AT WHERE YOU'RE HEADED, AS WELL AS WHERE YOU'VE BEEN

In my line of work, there are coaches, authors, and speakers who are all ahead of me in terms of experience and achievements. They have conducted more hours in meetings with clients and thus have had more coaching experiences that went great, as well as more experiences that did not go as well. They have written more books, more blogs, more podcast recordings. Some have implemented processes and programs faster to help their business grow.

If I only look at those ahead of me, I can get discouraged. But I can see a similar difference if I look at people who are "behind me," which is something most of us rarely do. I can see that I have more coaching hours under my belt than some competitors, that I've had more speaking engagements, released more podcast episodes, and so on. Progress simply takes time. Experience happens little by little.

So today as you build your business, don't get frustrated because you are not yet where you want to be, or where you believe your competitors are. You are on a journey. This is also true of your personal life.

If others look like they are doing better in their marriage or as a parent, that's probably because that person has spent more hours communicating with God or incorporating Him into their family.

Do not be discouraged by where you are at today in comparison to others. Instead, decide what you can do today to start progressing, little by little, toward where you want to be.

Have faith that God is just in front of you, clearing the path. Don't try and run around Him and blaze your own trail. And don't get frustrated and just choose to sit down on the path.

Instead, follow closely behind Him while making sure you are doing the part that is yours: building the business infrastructure, the family rhythms, and the character foundation that will prepare you to handle the new territory God is helping you conquer.

ACTION STEPS

Spend five minutes thinking about areas in your life (both at work and at home) that are causing you frustration because you are not as far along as you would like.

- Is your marriage stale? Maybe the action is to schedule a date.
- Rough relationship with a child? Maybe the action is to go and get ice cream together.
- Is your business pipeline low? Maybe reach out to some potential prospects.

For each of these items, write out a "little by little" step you can take to grow that area, and then block out a time in your schedule to do it.

PRAYER

Lord, I repent for all the times I've wanted to blaze my own trail, and for those times when I've thought that you moved off my path and were helping other people instead. I know that you are helping me and clearing my path. I pray that I will be focused on my own business, my own life, and my own path today and not looking at other people's paths. Thank you for plowing the land before me. Amen.

23

HOW ARE YOU MARKING THE MOMENT?

Leadership Trait: Celebration

1 Samuel 7:12, "Then Samuel took a stone and set it up between Mizpah and Shen and called its name Ebenezer, for he said, 'Till now the Lord has helped us.'"

Last year my oldest daughter, Kiley, came with me on a road trip I took for my work, and along the way, we visited three college campuses. One of the colleges we visited was Clemson University. As a college football fan, I enjoyed seeing this campus and football stadium because Clemson has been a top-tier program for years.

While we were at the football stadium, we had the opportunity to see the famous "Howard's Rock." This large piece of quartzite was given to Coach Frank Howard by a friend in 1966. The friend had hoped Coach Howard could find a use for it. But he couldn't, and so the rock sat in his office for over a year. Finally,

Coach Howard decided he wanted it out of his office, so he told an employee he could do whatever he wanted with it.

The employee then drove around campus for a few hours and finally decided to put the rock on top of the hill at the east end zone of the stadium. In the very next game, Clemson came back from an 18-point deficit to defeat Virginia! Thanks to that come-from-behind victory, Clemson decided to make a pedestal for the rock and leave it at that location permanently for good luck!

On September 23, 1967, the football players on the team rubbed the rock for the first time, and they ended up winning that game as well! To this day, the players still gather around Howard's Rock and touch it before they run down the hill at the start of all their home games.

Other colleges have similar traditions. Before each of their games, Notre Dame football players slap a sign that says "Play Like a Champion Today" as they run out of their locker room and onto the field. These traditions endure because, often, they work. They don't work because there is power in the Clemson rock itself or in the Notre Dame sign. The power lies in what the action does to the mindset of the player who touches the rock or sign.

Stuart Vyse, former professor of psychology at Connecticut College and author of *Believing in Magic: The Psychology of Superstition,* explained in an interview with the British Psychological Society, "These performance benefits are produced by changes in perceived self-efficacy. Activating a superstition boosts participants' confidence in mastering upcoming tasks, which in turn improves performance."[15]

Granted, there may occasionally be a player who doesn't care and who nonchalantly touches the rock and does not feel moved. But most of the time, for most players, the act delivers a psychological dopamine hit. These players are visualizing past successes and

15 Stuart Vyse, quoted in "How Do Superstitions Affect Our Psychology and Well-Being?," *Medical News Today*, September 13, 2019, https://www.medicalnewstoday.com/articles/326330#How-superstitions-may-relieve-anxiety.

leveraging the idea that they—as individuals and as a team—have been in this situation before. They have won in the past and they will win again. They are getting infused with the idea that other players on their team, and in their school history, are winners. All of this collectively helps get them in the right headspace for the game.

The same is true for you and me. No, we are not playing football. But in a sense, business and life are games too, and we need to put forth our best effort. We can play passively and get steamrolled by the demands of work or crying toddlers. Or we can be victorious in our efforts to build our businesses and families.

I love the story in 1 Samuel 7 because it shows how the Israelites created *their* pregame tradition using a stone of remembrance and how that practice can help all of us. In this chapter, the Israelites had just won a battle thanks to a literal act of God. We read in verse 10 that the "Lord thundered with a mighty sound that day against the Philistines and threw them into confusion, and they were defeated before Israel."

The Israelites were outnumbered, so for them to be victorious, God had to blind and confuse the Philistines. The Israelites were so grateful for this victory, and they were so in awe of God's involvement, that afterward they built an Ebenezer. An Ebenezer is something physical that reminds people of something spiritual that took place—a reminder that something happened that could only have happened due to an act of God.

In the case of the Israelites, the Ebenezer was a stone statue. You and I also experience these God moments in our lives, and we need to build a few Ebenezers in our environments to mark those moments. That way, when we are in a rut or in a low spot on our "Up and to the Right" graph, our Ebenezers can remind us that we have been in a low spot before, and that God got us out of those spots and will do it again!

WHAT IS YOUR EBENEZER?

Around my office I have a few Ebenezers. Among them is a custom-made wood sign with a phrase that has meaning to me, a few rocks picked up in Montana during significant quiet times in which I heard from God, and a few cards and notes of encouragement from loved ones and clients.

My friend and client Lucas Cole, CEO of Epipheo, has an Ebenezer in his office as well. About fifteen years ago, Lucas was living in Cincinnati and had just accepted a promotion to move back to Detroit. Soon after accepting the job, Lucas sensed that God did not want him to take this new job, and in fact wanted him to stay in Cincinnati—but for what Lucas did not know at the time.

Justifying the significantly higher pay raise, company car, and even a signing bonus, Lucas made a deliberate choice to ignore God's promptings and continued with the process of even signing an apartment lease in Detroit. Lucas tried to reason with God that he would find a new church in Detroit and get very involved.

However, there was a significant turning point that came for him while bowling with a mentee of his. They had been discussing the pros and cons of this move, and in the spirit of fun and wanting to see if God would give Lucas a sign, they decided to take the matter to bowling! They said that if Lucas knocked down more pins on the next ball than his friend, then he would proceed with his move to Michigan. However, if the mentee knocked down more pins, then Lucas would stay in Cincinnati.

Lucas went first and knocked down nine pins! Odds were very good that Lucas would be moving to Michigan!

Next, it was the mentee's turn. Up to that point in the night, he had not knocked down more than three pins in a single roll. The outcome appeared to be final. However, to both men's surprise and excitement, the mentee hit a strike!

The bowling test shook Lucas and even made him wonder if he should open his ears back up to God and consider not moving to Detroit. That night, Lucas could not sleep, and at 1 a.m. he desperately prayed and heard very clearly that God did not want him to take the promotion, and even that he should leave that employer because God had something else for him.

Lucas had no idea at the time what God had planned for him, but the very next day he rejected the offer and resigned from that employer, trusting God for what was next!

I don't generally recommend using bowling to make big life decisions. However, it clearly had an impact on Lucas. And in the days that followed, Lucas received even more confirmations that he should stay in Cincinnati.

Today, to mark the moment, Lucas keeps a bowling pin on his office shelf to memorialize the decision to stay in Cincinnati and pursue his calling. Since that night, it has become increasingly clear that God was involved in that decision. Lucas has gone on to be very involved in the entrepreneurial ecosystem in Cincinnati, involved in a few startups, and now is CEO of Epipheo, which makes explainer videos for companies, and employs over thirty-five people! As CEO, Lucas recently led the company through a sale that made them an ESOP (Employee Stock Ownership), or employee-owned company. This means that the employees benefit directly from the growth and profits of the company.

Where has God had a major impact in your life? Where has He helped you go from a valley to a peak? I encourage you to find or create an Ebenezer that marks that moment so you can increase in your confidence in knowing God is with you and be reminded that together you have conquered difficult times.

ACTION STEPS

List at least three big moments in your life, both good and bad. After you're done, spend some time thinking through those moments and list the ways God was involved, whether through His provision, through a divinely appointed connection, or through some other hard-to-explain circumstance.

Now create or find some physical object that you can put in

your office to remind you of a moment (or moments) when God was with you. It doesn't matter what object you use. It can be a rock, a painting, or even a framed print of an inspirational phrase or saying. The only thing that matters is that the object has meaning to you.

Also, spend time celebrating these prior wins! Once you come up with your Ebenezer, tell your work team and family what it is and explain why you chose it. As you move forward and encounter new wins, celebrate them with your family and your work team in ways that feel joyful to you.

BONUS: RISE AND GO MANIFESTO

The material you wrote down for your action steps in this chapter can be a great addition to the part 6, "God Has the Nightshift" section of your manifesto. Make sure to review this section from time to time! List some ways you have seen God show up in your life, both personally and professionally.

PRAYER

God, thank you so much for helping me through the difficult times. I am grateful for the times you helped me for which I've made an Ebenezer. I am grateful, too, for all the times you helped me that I simply just remember. I am also grateful for the times you helped me that I've already forgotten as well as those I didn't give you credit for because I thought I did it all! I pray that I will be more aware of your involvement and movements in my life and less self-focused, thinking that what needed to be done was all on me. Thank you for always being there for me. Amen.

CONCLUSION

My prayer is that if you read this entire book, then you no longer feel stuck. You are, in fact, in a season of breakthrough. Amen! Well done.

Though you've finished *Rise and Go*, I encourage you to continue to stick with the habits of quiet time, prayer, and spending time in the Word that you've been practicing while reading this book. Whether you read in the morning, during your lunch hour, or at night, keep that time sacred going forward so you don't fill it with other stuff!

Remember what Paul talks about in Romans 7:15: "For I do not understand my own actions. For I do not do what I want, but I do the very thing that I hate." We are all a lot like Paul. If we break out of our good habits and disciplines, then the desires of the flesh will creep back in and we will start to pick up some of our old bad habits and mindsets again. So keep pressing forward. Stay diligent in this effort to *Rise and Go*.

It's a lot like working out. Whenever we take a few weeks off, we get soft. Don't let your mind get soft.

Most importantly, as you move on from here, remember that you are blessed! No matter the size of your income or house, and no matter what your situation is, you are blessed. You are alive and leading people at your work and in your home. You have friends and family who love you. You are a beloved son or daughter of God.

If you are like me, you may find that it's easy to take all you have for granted. But I encourage you to be like the one leper who was cleansed and gave thanks, instead of the other nine. I'm referring to the story in Luke 17 that tells of the time Jesus entered a village and was met by ten lepers who asked to be healed. Jesus healed all ten of them, but only one turned around and gave thanks!

> Luke 17:15–16 "Then one of them, when he saw that he was healed, turned back, praising God with a loud voice; and he fell on his face at Jesus's feet, giving him thanks."

Can you believe that only *one* turned around to say thanks? Can you believe the other nine just walked away and carried on with their lives?

I find that truth shocking. But then—*oh wait!* I remember that all too often, I am one of the nine! I don't always tell God thanks for the good in my life. I am certain that there are times when I take my blessings for granted and just stay focused on the busyness of life.

Even Jesus was surprised that only one turned around to say thanks. In verse 17, He said: "Were not ten cleansed? Where are the nine?"

As I wrote this book and worked with my clients, I was prompted to remember more clearly all the good there is in my life. I felt prompted to turn around and thank God for all that He has given me and all that He has done for me: both in the good times and in the times I have been knocked down. My hope and prayer is that reading this book does the same for you.

Finally, Jesus said to the healed man words that I think we can all live by. It is the message we started with, and the message we have been moving toward throughout this whole book.

> Luke 17:19, "And he said to him, "Rise and go your way; your faith has made you well."

Thank you for reading. Rise and go!

RISE AND GO MANIFESTO

Throughout this book, I have made references to the Rise and Go Manifesto that I have been using in my own life for the last couple of years. I want to provide you with an explanation of how I built mine so you can use it as a framework to build something similar. You can view a sample version at www.corymcarlson.com/riseandgo, but I've also included a summary of the various parts below.

Scan the QR code to find additional Rise and Go resources

I am not the first person to come up with the idea of reading a daily document. However, I am now a huge fan of using one. I built my Rise and Go Manifesto framework using ideas I gathered from various sources, including mentors in my life and books. Chris Hartenstein shared the idea of the Identity Prayer in an exercise that was used at his New Frontier ministry experience in Montana years ago. I learned about the Morning Formula used by Taylor Welch, cofounder of Traffic and Funnels, when I went through his company's coaching program. The idea of "I am" statements is not a new idea, however, I have used "I am, I will, and I do not" statements to help drive myself and my clients toward their goals.

Great mindset books, such as *Psycho-Cybernetics* by Dr. Maxwell Maltz and *177 Mental Toughness Secrets of the World Class* by Steve Siebold, included stories and scientific evidence that further confirmed for me the value of using this type of routine. All these elements contributed to the development of my manifesto. Feel free to modify my example in any way that will help to motivate and inspire you.

One word of caution: I have been working with this manifesto for almost two years, and I have added and removed parts along the way. This is a living document. So give yourself grace as you build your own manifesto. Doing this work takes time, and your manifesto does not have to be perfect. As a matter of fact, it doesn't have to motivate or inspire anyone but *you*!

PART 1—IDENTITY PRAYER

God has an unlimited amount of character traits. He is just, loving, compassionate, a provider, merciful, and so much more. Yet each person will resonate with some of His character traits more than with others. For example, knowing that God is my provider gives me more peace than it might give someone else. Remembering His provision helps me on days I feel the weight of my job and the responsibility of providing for my family.

Spend time writing out all of God's character traits that mean something to you. When you're done, turn them into sentences and write a prayer that asks God to help you know who He is and what He is telling you each day.

PART 2—IDENTITY BIO

There are days when I wake up with doubts and I feel insecure about who I am and what I do. The purpose of this section of the manifesto is to record who I am, what I am currently working on, and where in my life I can currently find successes. Reviewing it helps me to shake off any doubts Satan is trying to instill in me. My identity starts with the fact that I am a son of God, and then it flows into my family, my work, and what I do each day.

Spend time writing out what you do and who you are. This may feel a bit like writing a resume at first. But this list can help you to remind yourself of your current successes: your job title, your responsibilities at work, your roles in your family and in the community, and more. These identities are what we use to live out all that God has called us to do.

PART 3—"I AM" STATEMENTS

There are days when I hear lies in my mind. I like to refer to these as head trash, as I further explain in my book, *Win at Home First*. If I am not careful, I will accept those lies and start to believe them! In Luke 4 we read that Jesus defeated Satan's three temptations in the wilderness by using God's truth from the book of Deuteronomy. We need to do the same. In this section, I identified common lies that I hear, but then use truth to defeat that lie. I then support that truth with a Bible verse.

For example, there are days when I feel that I am defined by a bad month. So in my Rise and Go Manifesto I have written, "I am building a business. A bad day does not mean that God is abandoning me."

I then follow that statement up that with a Bible verse: *"Keep your life free from love of money, and be content with what you have, for he has said, 'I will never leave you nor forsake you'"* (Hebrews 13:5).

Spend time listing some of the common lies you tell yourself and negative thoughts that you have. Next, write out the truth that defeats that lie. Finally, research and write down Bible verses that support that truth.

PART 4—WHAT I WANT

In chapter 4 of this book, we talked about the time Jesus asked the disciples, "What are you seeking?" This section is meant to visually capture what *you* are seeking. It is the vision board section of the document. In my own manifesto, I have added pictures of goals that I have set for myself and my life. For example, I want to take each of my kids on a mission trip. So I have a picture of Nicaragua in this section (which is where I went on the first mission trip with one of my children).

Spend time thinking about what you want. Next, look for pictures you can use to create a vision board, and then add them to your manifesto to help you envision what you are dreaming and praying for.

PART 5—HOW I WILL GET THERE

Having a vision board is great, but we also need to have some habits and rules that will help us get to where we want to go. We need a framework for success. In this section of my manifesto, I have listed tasks that I will and will not do in order to be successful. For example, I have written down that I will do both my quiet time and exercise at least four times per week. I also have written that I will not drink after 8 p.m. on weeknights, as I know that makes me less effective the next day.

Spend time thinking about the tasks and habits you need to start doing and stop doing in order to be successful and reach your goals. Next, add these "I will and I do not" statements into your manifesto.

PART 6—GOD HAS THE NIGHTSHIFT

In this section of my manifesto, I have listed the weird and wild stories from my life that only happened because God was involved. Whenever I read these, I am reminded that I am not alone on my journey!

This section is my reminder that God has the nightshift of my business and my life. For example, about ten years ago, I volunteered once at my church's Kids Club, and while I was there I met a woman named Kim Botto, who ran Kids Club at the time. Kim ended up submitting my name to my church's leadership team as a potential participant in a two-year leadership program that church employees and selected volunteers would go through. I had zero involvement in putting my name in that hat. Yet this leadership program is how I learned of Brandon Schaefer, who eventually became my coach.

Spend some time reflecting on your life and business. List some things that could only have happened because God was involved. Put these stories in your Rise and Go Manifesto. I further encourage you to create an Ebenezer for some of these events and put them in your office or home to help remind you of God's impact in your life.

PART 7—I HAVE WON BEFORE

Some days, we just don't think we have what it takes to be successful. As a matter of fact, we forget that we already *have been* successful. This section of my manifesto captures the times in my life when I have succeeded and experienced wins. I have listed various sales awards I've won and trips I've taken throughout my career. When I read this list, I am reminded that I have experienced success before, and I begin to believe that I will do so again!

Spend some time listing titles, awards, or other kinds of recognition you have had in your life, and put them into your manifesto.

PART 8—QUOTES

This section is a collection of quotes and phrases that I have heard that remind me of aspects of life and leadership that are important. My own manifesto includes quotes from John Maxwell, Warren Buffet, and many others. I even include anonymous quotes that I find helpful.

Spend some time writing down your favorite quotes and inspirational statements for this section of your manifesto. Here is one quote from my manifesto that may inspire you to take action on any of the ideas you have had while reading this book.

Mark Batterson, pastor and *New York Times* Bestseller, says in his book *The Circle Maker*, "But if you aren't willing to step out of the boat, you'll never walk on water. If you aren't willing to circle the city, the wall will never fall. And if you aren't willing to follow the star, you'll miss out on the greatest adventure of your life."[16]

Time to Rise and Go!

---

16 Mark Batterson, *The Circle Maker: Praying Circles Around Your Biggest Dreams and Greatest Fears* (Grand Rapids: Zondervan, 2011), 48.

ACKNOWLEDGMENTS

Holly—Thank you for encouraging me when I needed it. Thank you for also speaking truth to me when I needed it, even if it wasn't what I wanted to hear at the time! Thanks for being a great wife and mother, and for allowing me to pursue this dream. ILU.

Kiley, Kamdyn, and Kaleb—Thank you for being such incredible kids. I am grateful for your support and your grace, as I know I can be "too coachy" at times!

Dad and Jo—Thanks for being incredible parents. Thanks for all the encouragement you have given me and the prayers you have prayed as I have grown the business and my family.

Ron and Veda—Thanks for your love and encouragement.

To my family: Carlsons, Davisons, and Sheltons—thank you all for the love and support on this journey!

My past and current clients—Thank you for our conversations, which have made me a better coach and leader. Thank you for putting your faith in my leadership and for your support of my business. I can't believe that I get to do this for a living, and that I get to work with inspiring people like you!

Brandon Schaefer and Five Capitals—Thank you for being my coach and for your timely wisdom and insight over the last decade.

Brian Tome and Crossroads Church—Thank you for the teachings, devotions, social media posts, and other media that have helped me and my family grow closer to God over the last few years.

"Win at Home First" podcast guests—It is wild how God works, because the conversations I had with each of you were always very timely. Your wisdom and insight were always what I needed at that moment in my life, so thank you for your support and for being on the podcast.

My weekly leadership email readers—Thank you for your support and encouragement over the last couple of years as you read and provided feedback to the weekly content and stories I send out.

Friends who endorsed *Rise and Go*—I know endorsing a book is not an easy task as you must read the book and provide the endorsement, plus take the risk of associating your name with another book and author. Thank you for taking the time and risk!

My small group (aka "Wine Guys")—Thank you guys for providing me with community, encouragement, tons of laughs, and just the right amount of challenge during these last few years to keep pushing me forward.

Shari MacDonald Strong, Lois Stück, Olivia Nicodemus, Chad Reynolds, Shahbaz Qamar, Polly Letofsky, and Victoria Wolf— Thank you for your help and expertise to take *Rise and Go* from just an idea to an actual book and experience. Attention readers: if you are interested in writing a book and using any of these resources, please reach out to me and I can put you in contact with them.

Most importantly, God, thank you for letting me be a part of what you are doing. Thank you for giving me not just second chances, but a million chances!

To everyone else involved in my life but not listed above—thank you, too! I appreciate your smiles, your timely words of encouragement, your support on social media posts, prayers, and everything else you've done and continue to do for me. I couldn't do all this without you.

Thank you.

NEXT STEPS

Bring the proven success principles from *Win at Home First* or *Rise and Go* to your business or organization. Or have Cory customize a keynote address, workshop, or other talk on the topics of purpose, priorities, culture, or the Enneagram to meet your specific needs.

To work with Cory or invite him to speak at your next event, email cory@corymcarlson.com or visit www.corymcarlson.com/speaking.

Join other business leaders who receive weekly insight and ideas by subscribing to Cory's weekly email at www.corymcarlson.com.

COACHING AND SPEAKING ENDORSEMENTS

COACHING

"Cory brings an energy and enthusiasm with a perspective that's very unique to executive coaching. If you're considering a coaching relationship, I would highly recommend networking with Cory and exploring how he can help you take your game to the next level!"

—JT TURBA, Managing Partner, Vaco

"I have worked with Cory for a couple of years and highly recommend him to any business leader looking for a business coach. The most beneficial piece was he helped elevate my mindset to be the CEO of decent size architecture firm and encouragement to keep growing."

—DALE DIBELLO, Owner, Dibello Architects

"Having Cory as a coach has helped me greatly, both in terms of my professional development as a leader and at home. He helps keep me balanced and positive, and focused on seeing the opportunities in all situations. I highly recommend working with Cory."

—MATT BOWTELL, President, Terelion

"The impact that Cory has had on my personal and professional development is amazing. I've been challenged in many ways to step out, but more importantly to step up to who God is calling me to be at work and at home. Not only will you see a ROI on your life, but so will those around you."

—FRANCISCO MORALES, Director of Operations, Fry the Coop

"Cory brings a wealth of real-world experience and a sound biblical foundation. He has helped me with my communication (up/down), organization, prioritization, confidence, and overall leadership. If you are considering using an Executive Coach I highly recommend Cory!"

—**KRISTIAN STANKIEWICZ**, Vice President, Ameri-Kart

"Cory has been instrumental in helping me establish daily structure, discipline, and balance by equipping me with tools and resources to grow and better lead my teams."

—**WILL MACKIE**, General Manager, Azelis Americas CASE

"I would not have experienced this growth without Cory's coaching. Cory has helped me grow my business by more than 100% YOY. His coaching helped me to identify specific and measurable goals for the year."

—**STUART TATTUM**, Partner, Columbus Consulting

"Before Cory, I had never considered executive coaching. However, he has been instrumental in helping me navigate a toxic work environment, grow my emotional intelligence, and see opportunities where I believed none existed."

—**RYAN WALKER**, Senior Vice President,
Federal Affairs at Shumaker Advisors Ohio

"One of the most solid leadership coaches I've ever met. He helped our team identify issues and figure out a practical plan to get on track. I highly recommend him!"

—**RENJI BIJOY**, Founder & CEO, Immersed

"Cory has been my coach for over three years. I attribute so many of the personal and professional breakthroughs I've had during this time to his insight and counsel."

—**NICK SPICHER**, Vice President — Kroger Team, The Harvest Group

"In a world where most coaches only pay lip service to personal growth, Cory stands out. He has made me not only a better business man, but a better man."

—**BEN BESHEAR**, CEO & Private Wealth Advisor at LiveWell Capital — Northwestern Mutual

SPEAKING

"Our company session went great. Received several compliments on how much the talk helped people re-calibrate their minds that are usually so focused on work performance. This is a message that should resonate with almost any leader, and Cory does a great job delivering it."

—**DAN CALONGE**, Head of Learning & Development, Altafiber

"Cory was a well-prepared and engaging speaker. He had high energy, great questions and framework for guests to work through, and lots of additional complementary resources for attendees. I also really enjoyed his book *Win at Home First!*"

—**SAMANTHA FISHER**, Engagement Specialist, Thrivent Financial

"Cory gave our leadership group and our team members a motivating message that will have a lasting impact on each of us personally and for our businesses. I highly recommend him. His style allows his message to be absorbed. He is a man of strong character who can help you or your team just like he did ours."

—**RYAN POWELL**, Chief Operating Officer
and Owner, Vison Source Eyecare

"Cory came to my company to speak to our sales and operations team. He did an outstanding job and his message really hit home with our group. In our busy lives, it is easy for things to come out of balance. His message of the five capitals and winning at home was refreshing and timely."

—**TODD ALBRECHT**, Owner and President, Perfection Group

"Listeners always walk away from Cory's workshops with greater knowledge and insight into how they're forming their identities. He's an engaging speaker who knows how to connect with people on a deeper level that actually inspires and motivates the hearers to action."

—**LUKE DOOLEY**, President, OCEAN

"Cory was engaging, vulnerable, and inspirational. I highly recommend having Cory speak to your leadership team, because we all can lead better at home and work!"

—**MARSHALL HYZDU**, President at
Archbishop Moeller High School

ALSO BY CORY M. CARLSON

Win at Home First is a practical, eye-opening guide that helps business leaders, entrepreneurs, and executives learn how to thrive both at work and home.

"Spot on. Transformational for the individual who wants to be a positive leader." - **JON GORDON**, best-selling author of *The Power of Positive Leadership* and *The Carpenter*

WIN at HOME FIRST

AN INSPIRATIONAL GUIDE TO WORK-LIFE BALANCE

CORY M. CARLSON

Foreword by **BRIAN TOME**, Founder and Senior Pastor of Crossroads Church and author of *The Five Marks of a Man*

Many business leaders focus on winning at work. Driven by our own fear or by the expectations of others, we put pressure on ourselves to succeed. Then we give whatever time and energy we have left to our family and to ourselves. In the end, no one wins. Your relationships suffer, your kids are neglected, your teams at work are not developed, and you are not fulfilled.

There is a better way. You, your home, and your work can all thrive. This book will help you discover how to:

- Craft a personal and family vision
- Achieve work/rest balance
- Have a close relationship with your spouse and a marriage filled with fun and intimacy
- Build into your kids to set them up for success in life
- Prioritize for even greater impact at work
- Equip and empower your employees

Succeeding at work doesn't mean you have to fail at home. You can do both. Learn how with *Win at Home First*.

Win at Home First was an Amazon #1 New Release in 3 categories and listed in *Forbes* as one of "7 Books Everyone on Your Team Should Read."

ABOUT THE AUTHOR

As an entrepreneur, former executive, husband, and father of three, Cory Carlson understands the pressures working parents face. He is passionate about helping business leaders win at home and work.

Twenty years in corporate America gave Cory amazing opportunities as he worked his way up to the executive level. But he also saw brokenness all around him: work without purpose, burnout, lack of focus, strained marriages, and absentee parents. Business leaders especially were often not living life to the fullest.

When Cory began to work with a coach, he became a better leader, husband, and father. So he left his corporate career to help other leaders achieve a healthier work-life balance too. Cory currently lives in Cincinnati with his awesome wife and three amazing children.

Cory has a Civil Engineer degree from University of Missouri and an MBA from Rockhurst University. His first book, *Win at Home First*, is an inspirational guide for work-life balance. It was Amazon's #1 New Release in three Categories in June 2019 and was listed in *Forbes* as one of "7 Books Everyone on Your Team Should Read." He hosts the leadership podcast, *Win at Home First,* a top 1.5 percent global podcast per ListenNotes.

Follow Cory on social media (@carlsoncory) and www.corymcarlson.com.

Made in the USA
Monee, IL
04 October 2023

43963357R00116